My Fifty Years in Seattle's
Medical-Dental Building

A Brief History of
the Building and Me.
1958-2008 and More

Sam Goto

Book Publishers Network

Book Publishers Network
P.O. Box 2256
Bothell · WA · 98041
PH · 425-483-3040

Copyright © 2011 by Sam Goto

All rights reserved. No part of this book may be reproduced, stored in, or introduced into a retrieval system, or transmitted in any form or by any means (electronic, mechanical, photocopying, recording, or otherwise) without the prior written permission of the publisher.

10 9 8 7 6 5 4 3 2

Printed in the United States of America

LCCN 2010914847
ISBN10 1-935359-68-1
ISBN13 978-1-935359-68-5

Cover designer: Laura Zugzda
Typographer: Stephanie Martindale

Contents

Acknowledgements

My wife, Dee worked to correct my spelling and put a little more order to the pages because I drew and wrote down my thoughts as they came to me this past year or two – in no particular order. Thanks to everyone who gave me stories, encouraged me and specially to David Branch who gave the book a once over.

Forward

Sam started working in the Medical-Dental Building for Dr. Sproule in 1958. I came into the picture after we married in 1961. One night, I was home alone, as usual because of his long hours, ironing his T-shirts. Wives used to do things like that in those days. I was wondering what I would do if something happened to Sam. A few nights before a dental technician had hit a freeway barrier because he was exhausted from overwork and died. Sam had warned me about the high mortality of his trade and that was why he married a nurse. Since that time, I learned to appreciate our life together and the lifestyle we have because of his work ethic.

As a result of his talents and commitment to his patients, Sam has drawn a reputation of being one of the best craftsmen in his field. Therefore, his work is found in the mouths of many of the leading citizens of Washington State and as far as Australia, Japan, Europe and Nova Scotia.

It is a business development fact that staying in the "Building & Creating" mode is essential. In 1925 when the Medical-Dental Building was first built, it was part of the progressive outskirts of the original city. In 1950 new construction doubled its size. In the 1990s Nordstrom relocated to the former Frederick & Nelson space to keep the area a thriving destination. In 2005 there was a major remodel of the building itself. Through the years the building continues to be the prestigious place for health related professional services and advice.

From 1969 to 2005, Sam had a window on the 4th floor, overlooking the front door of the Westin Hotel, where most of the world dignitaries came. He came home weekly with stories

viii   My 50 Years in Seattle's Medical-Dental Building

of what he witnessed. Now, he is on the 8th floor and is less bothered, but pleased to be next door to Michael Medved, national talk show host.

Sam says: "These stories are my personal perspective of my experience and stories told to me as I've worked for more than 50 years in the 'Medical-Dentical Building' as our young children used to call it. I figure I will write this for myself & my family. If others enjoy it, that is a bonus."

I love his stories, life lessons & art work and trust you will too.

-Dee Goto

1
The Beginning Years

In the summer of 2003, while checking a shade for a bridge on Shirley McCarter, I mentioned I was thinking of writing a book about the Medical-Dental Building (M-D Bldg). She got excited and said she had an announcement of her father's when he had started practice here in 1926 after moving from the Cobb Building.

Dr. Robert C. McCarter's office was 921. Shirley was his assistant before she became a dental hygienist.

His son, Robert G, joined his dental practice after graduation from the U of W School of Dentistry in 1952.

In 1922 a group of dentists and physicians got together to establish a "real" medical center in Seattle. It was largely a protest against inadequate facilities and unjust rental prices. One doctor reported rent being raised from $75 to $215 per month.

LOCATION MUST BE IDEAL – "The location is the choicest in the city, as there are more streets intersecting around this block than any other downtown point"

-1925 M-DBLDG Bulletin

WWI had ended and the 1918 Spanish influenza epidemic was over. The Roaring Twenties ushered in a decade of easy credit and economic prosperity. Middle-class America grew and created a high demand for new products such as automobiles, phones, phonographs and radios. It was a time of optimism. Seattle's population was 315,000. Women could vote, Prohibition was on, but speak easies flourished...times were good!

This information is from the 1925 Souvenir Bulletin that all new tenants sent out to their patients.

The M-D Bldg was an eighteen story building designed by John A. Creutzer. Each floor had the capacity of thirty-two offices.

The sixth floor had a fifteen bed Hospital, staffed by graduate nurses.

Built by Bradner Building Company. Owned and operated by West and Wheeler.

The first phase of the M-D Bldg was completed for $2.5 million. This included the foundation and walls to support Phase Two on the 6th Avenue side, to be built later. The 1925 souvenir announcement listed 125 Doctors of Medicine and 96 Doctors of dental surgery.

The building is fireproof terra cotta facing, a spacious lobby in Gothic style, bronze elevator doors, a lobby and walls of marble, Terrazzo floors and the interior finish is Bataan mahogany.

Costs were advertised as being about 20 percent less than most rentals doctors were paying elsewhere, with better accommodations!

"There is no other building of this character anywhere in the world as large or as beautiful as this, and nowhere has any project incorporated all the special accommodations for tenants and patients found in this structure."

-1925 M-D Bldg souvenier bulletin.

Entrance Lobby to the Medical and Dental Building, 1925

Elevator Lobby of the Medical and Dental Building, 1925

Speyer Gold Company – Bob & Leonard are some of my best sources of information for the history of the M-D Bldg.

The machinery didn't fit into the elevator, so they used the window!

Kirby Speyer was born in Kansas City, Missouri, in 1888. According to Bob, "Dad's folks originally came from Lexington, Kentucky, and they had a leather tanning business until it was sold. Then dad went to work for a Chicago Goldsmith, S.S. White Company, as a salesman. His family moved to Seattle when they sent him to manage a store here. Dad married Mom, Irna David – she was from Germany – here in Seattle about 1920. That was when people were dying of the big Spanish flu – Dad's mom died from it."

The 1928–'29 years, the M-D Bldg was bustling, new tenants were moving in and getting settled.

Plans were being made for the future expansion of the building but...

On October 29, 1929, the Roaring Twenties came to a roaring end – the stock market crashed. Panic! Black Tuesday!

Some people lost everything. People were reported to be jumping from buildings – none as far as I know from the M-D Bldg at that time.

The great Depression deeply affected everyone's life. Unemployment was way up. Business was way down. Soup lines were common. Many patients were paying their doctor bills with produce and in trade.

Half the banks failed during this depression, drained by panicked depositors. Money was scarce.

Dr. R. I. Vanderwall, one of the original dentists in the building, drove around the countryside to see some of his patients and to try to collect some money. Later, his son took over his practice and in turn sold it to Dr. David Branch in 1973 for $1500.

There was a story about one dentist that sneaked out of his U District dental office at night.

During those years, dentists often shared one receptionist. Business was slow - card games were easy to find.

In the early 1900s about the only Dental School around was in Portland, Oregon. Dr. Howard Gilbert tells about his dad graduating there as did Dr. Walter Sproule - John Sproule's Dad.

Dr. Howard I Gilbert is listed as one of the original tenants in the 1925 special souvenir bulletin.

Kelley-Ross Pharmacy was one of the early business tenants. John Oftebro - owner since 1973 - says, "Kelley and Ross were in competition to get into the lucrative M-D Bldg. They were the foremost prospects and finally agreed on a partnership."During the second generation of the Kelley and Ross families ownership, they were the largest prescription pharmacy in the United States.

Seattle's Shantytown of fifty shanties was first built within a few days the fall/winter of 1931-'32, just south of Pioneer Sqaure. Seattle Police burned it down a couple times but the city finally relented. March 1934 count included 632 men and 7 women living in 479 shanties.

"Hooverville" - named in sarcastic honor of President Hoover, blamed for the Great Depression

President Herbert Hoover's motto was "Prosperity is just around the corner."

PRES. HERBERT C. HOOVER
1929 -1933

Nothing seemed to work. The causes were obscure. Some thought it was oversupply; others over leverage.

PRES F.D. ROOSEVELT
1933-1945

President Roosevelt's motto was "The only thing we have to fear is fear itself."

My dad had finished his formal schooling in Japan and was sent to the United States to earn money to send one of the relatives to Medical School. He was fourteen years old in 1914 when he jumped ship in Tacoma and came in illegally. He was sworn to secrecy and died without telling anyone, even his wife, the details.

My mother was born in Barneston, now Cedar River Watershed, at a lumber camp. She was sent to Japan for her formal education - family was well off enough to be able to do this. Her dad was one of the Japanese dairy farmers that supplied half of Seattle's milk supply at one time. Returning to Renton, Mom was eighteen when a marriage to Dad was arranged by Dee's grandpa - we didn't know this until after we were married because the pioneer immigrants never talked about their hard times.

I was born during the heart of the great depression. My first memories are of living on a farm in Renton and thinking Mt. Rainier was on top of the clouds.

2
The War and Recovery Years

On December 7, 1941, Japan bombed Pearl Harbor in Hawaii, destroying planes and battleships!!

World War II had begun. War hysteria caused the incarceration of over 110,000 Japanese/Japanese Americans – 68 percent were American citizens. Leonard Speyer remembers when a lot of his classmates at Broadway High School were imprisoned at the Puyallup Fair Grounds and then sent to Minidoka in southern Idaho.

Here in Seattle, the war caused a shortage of workers, of gas and other basic necessities. Food was rationed. America mobilized for war. "'The Sleeping Giant' was awakened" – the phrase used by some behind the scenes officials in Japan who had been to the U.S. and knew how vast and developed we were. Not all were for attacking Pearl Harbor.

Dr. Olin Loomis told me in 2004 that he kept his office during the time he was in the service. Counting his WWII years he was in the M-D Bldg for over sixty years.

Worker shortage and moral was a problem, but Kirby Speyer hired a girl who wore tight sweaters and showed cleavage...

The Speyer boys served in the Navy. When Bob finished radio operator training, they needed a garbage truck driver in New Guinea – so that was part of his Pacific service between 1943-46.

Leonard and his brother Paul (1944) censored mail in Pearl Harbor for four to five months. Later in the Pacific, they were in Fire Control and took Marines into Iwo Jima on LSTs (Landing Ship Tanks). Leonard explains, "I saw some 'kamikazi' hits! Dad was glad to see us back alive."

(I had a cousin in Japan who was trained as a kamikazi pilot, but the war ended before he had to go. Dee and I visited him on one of our Japan trips. Interesting how they were trained to be blind followers of the Emperor; but post war, most of them respect us Americans and are grateful the US won.)

D-Day, June 6, 1944, Normandy Beach initiated V-E (Victory in Europe) Day. Following is a drawing of the famous photo by LIFE's Robert Capra of Omaha Beach. The soldier in the picture is Huston Riley who lives on Mercer Island where we have lived for thirty-seven years.

Not long ago our Mercer Island paper showed him being awarded a bottle of Omaha Beach Sand. This brings these world events close to our own lives.

President Roosevelt died on April 12, 1945, at age 63. As vice-president, Harry Truman became President and on May 7, 1945, Germany surrendered unconditionally.

August 6, 1945, a B-29, Enola Gay, dropped the atomic bomb on Hiroshima; initiating V-J (Victory in Japan) Day. The surrender papers were signed on September 2, 1945, on the battleship Missouri. We had a lot of relatives in Japan affected by that event.

In 1955, I was in the 95th Combat Engineer's Unit called: The Desert Rats - the same unit that tested the first atomic bomb.

My own family moved to Bully Creek in Eastern Oregon in 1937 to start over because of discriminatory problems in the Seattle area. We lived in a shack with no running water and a privy. So our family was in Eastern Oregon during the war years. Mom and Dad had seven children - Fred, Roy (died), me, Kiyo, Andy, Henry and Irene.

Although we were very poor, as kids didn't know the difference. Our parents made the best of their situations and were influenced by a heritage of Buddhism that believed in reincarnation and that we had chosen to be born into our situation to learn.

Time is teaching me - maybe it's easier to start at the bottom than starting at the top.

I learned about the end of the war surrender from a neighbor boy in Willow Creek, Oregon. Although Uncle Mush had visited us in a US armed forces uniform, I didn't realize a lot of the neighbors still considered us and him the enemy.

THE WAR IS OVER. YOUR UNCLE HAS SURRENDERED!

MY UNCLE IS IN THE U.S. ARMY!

His brother is Dave Wilcox – a Hall of Fame linebacker for the San Francisco 49ers.

WWII was over, life was returning to normal in Seattle. Doctors were returning to the M-D Bldg after their service. Thoughts again returned to expanding the building. A more modern expansion was planned.

Architect W. Henry Fey planned the improvement of the third floor east wing and relocation of the hospital there. Seattle papers carried the news.

In the late 1940s, the University of Washington started its dental school. The GI Bill made higher education possible for a lot of returning veterans. Two of the dentists recruited from Canada to help teach were Dr. John Sproule and Dr. Ken Morrison.

In 1950 the new expansion was completed. The addition added 100,000 sq. feet for a total of 290,000 sq. feet.

Meanwhile in Idaho, the war recovery years were difficult times for my family, but the moves gave me a chance to learn some of my most valuable life lessons. In 1947, I moved from Willow Creek, Oregon, to Weiser, Idaho, where as a freshman in high school and on the football team, I had a great coach,

In 1949, Dad was evicted from the Weiser, Idaho, farm and we moved again to Nampa, Idaho.

Coach "Babe" Brown showed me how important a good coach can be. His teams in basketball, football and baseball went undefeated. Our track team did okay.

"A good team is more than the sum of its parts!"

At the College of Idaho, I ran track with RC Owens, later to become famous as a San Francisco 49er. At a track meet in Salem, Oregon, R.C. Owen and I looked until we found a T.V. to watch the Jersey Joe Walcott fight.

After two years in college, I got my draft notice and decided to drop out and finish under the GI Bill, but I was a victim of the few years it became unavailable for veterans.

Brother Fred returned to Nampa after serving in the Korean War. Dad waited for his return and then moved the family to Quincy, Washington, Fall of 1953. Dad bought a three bedroom house for $10,000. It cost extra because we added a third bedroom for our family of eight.

Dad had gotten his citizenship the year before with the Warren/McCarren Act when non-whites and first generation Japanese were finally allowed to become citizens and own property.

In 1955 I was with Army's 95th Combat Engineers in Darmstadt, Germany. Then, I was called up to Stuttgart and the 7th Army Headquarters. I did charts for war games and NATO meetings in G-3 Operations. The men there were exceptional. In one of our many bull-sessions, Budro, who loved to philosophize, explained how he had escaped Russia with his scientist father and how US Army life was better than civilian life in Russia.

Discharged from the army in 1957, I decided to go into dental technology. My Uncle Ray Nakanishi was one of my mother's four brothers and had studied to be a dental tech in Los Angeles. He's the reason I got into the tooth business. While I was home that fall, I saw a UFO over the town of Quincy with lights resembling a wagon wheel. As I drove to Seattle, Russia had launched Sputnik. The Space Age had begun!!

When I got back from my two year stint in the Army, someone pretty special was taken. So, I let the disappointment empower me, and I was determined to do well in dental tech school. A cousin watched and commented that he thought I was always angry.

We've all had disappointments, and I've learned that one way to fight it off is to get angry. I figured this out when I watched President Eisenhower at a funeral. Anger may not always be appropriate, but it works for certain things.

Anger gave me direction and determination, It sure beat sitting around and feeling sorry for myself or being depressed. It gave me the guts to do somethings I was afraid to do and it's a good feeling to stand up for something you believe in. Right?

I came to Seattle in the fall of 1957, stayed with my sister Kiyo and enrolled in Al Jennings Dental Technician and Assistant School at 1018 2nd Avenue. I was one of three in his first class. The dental assisting part came in handy later too. In first grade, I was an only student in a one-room grade school in Bully Creek and claim I was the best in the class. Here, I was the only one to become a technician so I claim the same.

A girl in the class interviewed at the M-D Bldg and reported back. She didn't take the job. I later learned who it was.

My Uncle Ray Nakanishi was working for Dr. Doherty in the Cobb Building and heard about a dentist in the M-D Bldg that wanted an in-house technician.

So, in April of 1958, I interviewed for the job with Dr. Sproule at 1438 M-D Bldg. It was the first and last interview I've had. I wore the custom brown suit I had bought in Germany.

The first thing I learned was how to pour and pin models and how to trim them. Those firsts are seared into my memory.

3
Life in the Sixties

The Sixties have become synonymous with all the new, exciting, radical, and subversive events and trends of the period - Beatles, Kennedys, Moon Landing, Martin Luther King, Hippies. The World's Fair, Space Needle, Westin Hotel, Westlake Mall brought many celebrities by our M-D Bldg windows. For me, the Sixties brought marriage and family.

The average dentist made $15,576 in 1965 and translated to 1997 dollars, is $181,201.

In the 1960s, a few dentists and friends formed a slow pitch softball team. There were people like Phil Gallaher, Dick Iverson, Hersh Cox, Bob McCarter, Al Brown, Tom Simpson and the Speyer boys, who made up the M-D team. They called themselves the DKs (decay).

The building also sponsored some golf tournaments around that time.

Some dentists got together and formed a motorcycle group. They even motored all the way to the East Coast but came back by rail.

The Sproules took a six week trip to the Orient. I'd known Dee as a little girl in pigtails in Eastern Oregon and met again when she moved up to Seattle to get her Public Health Degree in 1960.

We were married at the First Baptist Church in Ontario, Oregon, on Christmas Eve 1961. That was the only day Dee's Uncles could take time off from their Ontario Market store. We left on a snowy night for our bridal suite, at an Idaho motel, in my '58 Ford. We hadn't eaten despite the marriage festivities and spent the early morning Christmas hours looking for place to eat. Finally, found a cop to help us find a place open.

We honeymooned down the West Coast, staying with relatives because we had more time than money. It was a good trip except for learning about California drivers when I got aced out of a parking place at Coit Tower in San Francisco and not being able to stay at one motel because of our race.

We watched the Space Needle being built for the 1962 World's Fair, built to withstand 200 mph winds and 9.1 magnitude earth quake. The 2001 Nisqually Earthquake sloshed the water out of the toilets but withstood the test. The Monorail added for the futuristic theme still runs with the terminal next to our building on 5th Avenue.

I remember seeing Elvis Presley (Wednesday, September 5, 1962) coming down the ramp of the Westlake Monorail station, carrying a child (Vicky Tiu). The movie Meet Me At The Fair was filmed here in Seattle. To see someone so famous in person is kind of fun. We enjoyed the Lennon Sisters and the Billy Graham Crusade at the stadium.

Most of us have seared in our memory what we were doing when President Kennedy was assasinated, November 22, 1963.

It was a usual Friday when Dr. Morrison was using Dr. Sproule's office for seeing private patients. The rest of the week he taught at the U of W Dental School. He was busy with a patient; I was in the next bay doing lab work.

I can listen to the radio while I work, but I have to concentrate so it's hard to talk. The sixties through the eighties, I listened a lot to Bob Hardwick and Jim French on KVI. Dee and I went to some of the community events they sponsored, like a camera seminar with Joseph Scalea. I enjoyed Helen Trump, "Down your street and up your alley."

TED GRIFFIN, 1965 !

Bob Hardwick piloted a tugboat to British Columbia to haul back Namu, the killer whale, for the Seattle Aquarium. He jet-skied 740 miles from Ketchikan to Seattle. He swam the Bremerton-Seattle ferry route.

Jim French was the creative writer – "Theatre of the Mind" was/is good. Cliff Murphy was the air traffic reporter and opened an antique business in Buckley and wanted an outhouse, so French agreed to build it and Ernst Hardware agreed to supply the precut material with a duplicate for the person who submitted the best design. I won his contest.

Tom Enbody sold shoes at Nordstrom before getting into tech work and talks about the advice he got from his boss, Elmer Nordstrom: "Remember to hire good help; bad help will ruin you every time." My Uncle Ray Nakanishi says Tom was the first dental tech he hired. Ray went on to develop Nakanishi Dental Lab - one of the largest in the Seattle area. Tom remembers when my uncle was looking for a house in different neighborhoods in the Seattle area at that time.

We have a street person who comes into the building and sits in the lobby. He wears a flowery skirt and a full beard. He gets around; I've also seen him in the U District. I wonder, what lessons in life bums are learning and what are we learning from them?

I asked a building maintenance person, Mark Rogers, what happened to his foot? It was in a cast. He said, "There were two street people urinating on our building, and I said, 'You shouldn't do that.' The next thing, I was flying upside down and a big black guy saved me!"

July 15, 1964, Dee said, "It's time." I called Dr. Lamkee. It was 2a.m. and I ran all the stop signs and lights I could but got no escorts to N.W. Hospital. Lynette was born at 5:41a.m.

Dr. Sproule warned me several times about not waiting too long. His first daughter was brain damaged when doctors held back the birth. He was bitter, but never thought of suing - he didn't like lawyers. Lynette's birth was normal and everyone was relieved. Dr. Sproule offered to be godfather for her.

Kelly's birth, October 26, 1967, was a different story. She came five weeks early. Dee's water broke, and police said they couldn't help. Neighbor, Penny Simkin, took Dee to the hospital. It was an emergency because of a detached placenta where most babies and half the mothers die.

Penny has since that time become world famous as a child birth educator and author.

Once when changing life insurances, we let it lapse. The reality of the children's birth caused me to be more careful and worry about the responsibility.

Like most mothers those years, Dee was a stay-at-home mom. We had one car and money was tight. The National Bank of Commerce (later Rainier Bank, Seafirst, and then Bank of America) across the street from the M-D Bldg, started a Christmas Club. I joined and put a few dollars in each month for Christmas presents. We didn't buy on credit those days. I was able to buy Dee an Omega watch for $80. That's expensive today.

Offices in the building were small. Most were only two bays. Other offices were expanding. I helped Sproule knock out walls and expand his office into three bays. The building management said they couldn't do it because it was a fire wall, but maintenance gave us advice and I learned a lot about remodeling.

It's been said businesses go through four phases.

1. Building and creating.

2. Managing.

3. Justification of no growth.

4. Quitting.

It's good to stay in the building and creating stage - even without getting physically larger. Dr. Sproule was like that; always thinking and trying new things.

The sixties were interesting times with marches and demonstrations, often coming by the M-D Bldg. One of the groups even came by our Capital Hill house on 23rd Avenue. East, starting at the U of W and marching all the way downtown. About that same time, I was awakened one night by a man shooting out the windows of a vacant building across 23rd Avenue, and I started thinking about moving.

Most parades came close to the building - Seafair royalty in new convertibles, pirates on their Pirate Duck Boat, Blue Angels roaring overhead. Our family used the office as headquarters for the Seafair Torch Light Parades.

Once in the late sixties, Sproule got a package from the Snohomish County Coroner. Inside was an envelope full of teeth. They wanted his help to identify a suicide victim. It was a patient for whom we had done a lot of gold work. She had drowned herself.

4
Learning From a Mentor

In the forties and fifties, I read a lot of comics - still do. Billy Batson's mentor was a wizard. Billy uttered the word SHAZAM! -the first letter of various Greek gods - and transformed into the mighty super hero, Captain Marvel. The strip was later shut down when lawyers said it was too much like Superman.

I learned a mentor was usually an older person who took a younger person under his or her wing to teach them the ropes of the business. It's a fast way of getting ahead and better than school learning. Mentors are usually among the best in their field. Dr. Sproule was my mentor. I was lucky!

He often said I knew more than most dentists. That was good of him and a good example of mentoring so I was motivated to do better because someone believed in me. But, like father and son - the son eventually wants to get on his own. I did. I was thirty-six years old. I opened my place April 1, 1969.

Shortly after I started working for him, Dr. Sproule called me into his operatory to look at a patient and showed me, in the patient's mouth, where to put a wire clasp on a partial. I did what I thought he explained. He was impressed and said it was perfect.

I made a lot of before and after models of full mouth cases using cold cure acrylic in Hydrocoloid molds. We made hinges out of coat hangers and painted the hinges and tops and bottoms.

Face to face, Sproule was tough; but sometimes late at night after dinner and a drink, he often called to discuss a case and to thank me for doing a good job.

Those days, smoking was in, and we took smoke breaks, discussing cases while looking at study models, working toward the ideal. Walls and ceilings got stained as well as my teeth.

I've heard there are two kinds of people; goal setters and problem solvers. I loved to tackle; defense is problem solving. I wasn't good at handling the ball but when I was in the "zone" I could be pretty good.

Sproule always said we both liked little problems. For instance, he had a lot of referrals of hard cases other dentists were afraid to touch. Most were full mouth cases.

He'd prep the whole mouth, keeping the vertical with good temporaries (metal and plastic); take face bow readings and mount on a dentatus articulator.

PATIENT WITH FACE BOW

QUOTE FROM U.W. PROF

After mounting the case on to the articulator and setting it to the readings, we had a good idea of how the patient's mouth functioned. It worked best when we got the vertical bite from the start. Opening and closing causes problems.

It could take all day of intensive work to wax-up a big case. We worked toward the ideal and tried a lot of techniques, but usually ended up with a modified Panky-Mann type occlusion - simple and worked well.

Dr. Sproule was good at theory and also very good with his hands. When he worked on you, you felt extra secure, and many patients, especially women, commented on it.

Sproule liked to figure out problems and help people he liked get ahead. He even offered to send me to dental school. I declined. I came in through the art end and felt my grades from the College of Idaho (now Albertson's) weren't good enough. Dr. Morrison taught at the Dental School and used Sproule's office once a week. He said he'd check it out, but never mentioned it again. I wonder.

There were plenty of problems, and I spent many nights doing things over. We had an acid heating pot that heated acid and let the fumes bubble through soda water so it would be safe of environmental toxicity when turned on. We used it to clean cements from bridges and remove long pin facings.

Nitric acid was used to eat away steel we used on some pin techniques. The other acid we used was hydrocloric acid. Once, after using nitric acid, I rinsed the pot and put in hydrocloric acid and ran the pot overnight. To our surprise, it ruined all the gold work. I was devestated. I had heard about aquaregia and looked it up. It was a combination of nitric and hydrochoric acids, only acid that could dissolve gold!

We used to use a lot of dangerous stuff. Another one was hydrofluoric acid, used to strip porcelain and clean contaminated metal. Once I stepped on a drop of acid in my stocking feet. It burned into my flesh and didn't stop till all its energy was gone.

Dr. Sproule was usually skeptical about new things. On dentures we used Frenche's lowers and rational uppers. Sometimes we used 30° uppers with Lingual into 20° lowers. But, when we were shown Centrimatics from Germany, he jumped right in. It used a plate on the uppers and a center poise ball bearing on the lowers. Adjustments were so good patients would say, "stop!" and we'd remove the stuff.

Dr. Sproule was always thinking about dentistry. On an over-night fishing trip to Black Lake with Jamie Pierre, son of "Little O'Bill Pierre" auto dealer in Lake City, Sproule looked at the Cascade Mountains and pointed out how they looked like teeth. "The grooves on teeth like streams on mountains don't intersect."

We hiked in five miles, carrying an inflatable boat and our camping gear. Sproule loved camping and the out-of-doors. I got to try out my new Orvis fly rod that he had given me for Christmas, but I didn't have much luck. Sproule was a good fly fisherman, but I could never get the hang of it.

One of his treasure finds was an old washing machine cover from Goodwill. He decided they made good presents and found several for his friends.

IMPARTING SOME
WISDOM DURING
SMOKE BREAKS.

Like a mentor, Sproule included me in some of his investment ideas. Once, we were out looking at property to invest with Leo Pierce, our accountant, Dr. Sproule included me in on some property that became Totem Lake. The investment turned out okay.

IN OTHER WORDS, DON'T
GET TOO GREEDY.

Another day, we had lunch in the Red Carpet Restaurant and invested money in Montgomery Mortgage, a company just being formed. I invested one thousand dollars, a lot for me at that time. More than a month's income. It failed!

Having lunch at Gene's Red Carpet on the street level of the M-D Bldg, was a special treat.

Dr. Sproule was a dentist's dentist, as was his father, Walter, in Vancouver, British Columbia, Canada. He always said, "I choose to be an American citizen!" The eleven years I worked in Sproule's office was always interesting because I got to meet the patients (twenty-two years total doing his lab work).

There was an old gentleman patient who had to use a voice amplifier to talk; he sounded like a robot. He was Dr. Ferrier, the famous "gold foil" man. There is a bronze bust of him at the U of W Dental School.

ABOUT 2 OZ. OF GOLD
A BELT BUCKLE

During my time in Sproule's office, I did other stuff besides lab work. I made a lot of belt buckles for his friends out of scrap gold. I also drew pictures and took photos for his study clubs.

We made a few string ties that were usually initials that were made to look like cattle brands.

PREGNANT! I NEED A RING!

Jo was his assistant when I first worked in Sproule's office. She was young and newly married. Her ring became contaminated with mercury and cracked. It got ruined when I tried to solder it. I made her a new ring. With Sproule's permission, I used some scrap gold.

Sproule liked to watch good waitresses. He watched Shirley at the Olympic Hotel and hired her. She learned quickly and ran the one girl office like it was her own business. She was good. He was always booked six weeks in advance and seldom confirmed appointments as it was an honor to be a patient. The patient paid half down and the rest on completion.

Shirley had retired, and I'd moved to my own place on the fourth floor. Dr. Sproule brought down a new girl for me to meet. Her name was Janna from Boise, Idaho. She was a single mom, lithe, and energetic. She lived at the Shorewood Apartments on Mercer Island.

Having built a new waterfront home in Kennydale, he found it convenient to pick Janna up and drop her off on his way to and from work.

One Monday morning, I ran into Sproule coming in late for work. He said, "I stopped this morning to pick up Janna as usual and she answered the door in the nude. So I took her to the hospital to have her checked out."

Janna did go back to school, and Sproule read me a poem he had written, "An Ode to Janna." It was a side of him I'd never known. It was good.

SHE HAD BEEN OUT OF IT 3 DAYS.

In February of 1980, Dr. Sproule brought back a small Schifflera plant in a lava rock for me from Hawaii. That was his last trip. Thirty years later, I keep the plant alive and trimmed like a bonsai.

I respected Dr. Sproule even though he called me "Boy" at times. He was thoughtful and even showed me where I was mentioned in his will - but never saw any of it.

In 1980, Dr. Sproule told me he wasn't feeling so good. A melanoma had been removed, he quit smoking and started playing racket ball. When I got back from summer vacation, he was in the hospital. Lung cancer had metastasized to his brain. He was cremated and his airline pilot friend, Russ Bath, spread Sproule's ashes over the M-D Bldg and over the mountains he so loved. He was fifty-eight years old.

5
Brushes With Fame

Dr. Bert Hagen was one of the original tenants. One day, he called me and wanted to know if I'd draw a skull. He actually wanted to show me one he'd done. It was good, like a da Vinci!

They called him "Boomer" because his booming voice could be heard down the hall. He wanted the "carriage" trade so he got to know a lot of famous people from all over the country.

Dr. Hagen even had a picture of himself with President Eisenhower, holding a golf score card, taken back in D.C. Hagen was a good athlete and was awarded the Perdy trophy, a fancy shot gun, for trap shooting from Mr. Perdy himself.

I spent quite a bit of time with Hagen, learning how he made porcelain inlays. First we made an amalgam die, then adapted platinum foil.

He talked about the day Bing Crosby came in for an emergency. Crosby was from Spokane, but evidently, his grandpa had been a lawyer in Seattle in the 1870s. Mr. Allen from Boeing was also a patient.

One of the last times I saw Dr. Hagen, he was in his lab taking pictures of the Orpheum Theatre being torn down! According to people in the know, the top floor held one of the finest brothels in Seattle. The largest brothel (Lester Apartments) was destroyed in 1951 by a B-50 Crash!

Dr. Hagen had a lot of memorabilia around that was always kind of fun. He was quite a womanizer or pretended to be as was considered manly in those days. A tragic aside, a girl who worked for him liked to change her shoes while sitting on the window sill. One day she fell out.

Dr. Branch took over the office when Hagen retired.

Pete Emt, director of St Vincent de
Paul for thirty years after its start
in 1926, always came in wearing a big
black hat, boots and a string tie. He
didn't look the part of a religious man
but he was. His big voice and manner
were misleading. One day he came in,
took off his big hat and had a black
smudge on his forehead. Sproule
wiped it off before starting work on
him, and only later realized it was a
religious day, Ash Wednesday.

Frank McLaughlin, president of Puget
Sound Power and Light Company
from 1931 to 1960, brought fancy,
expensive ties for Sproule and me
every Christmas. I still have one. We
made him a set of masculine dentures
that suited him well. He was most
appreciative and struck me as being
very devout.

Once when I was taking a shade on
Ralph Munroe, secretary of state,
1980 to 2001. I asked what he
did. He said, "I'm working on some
voter's pamphlets." I still didn't
know what his job was as he was
always joking. It made me think it
wasn't too important a job, and I'm
not sure I know more now.

In the 1950s and 1960s, Milton Katims was conductor of the Seattle Symphony Orchestra. The Katims were patients, and Mrs. Katims always wore her fur stole. Katims was a well-respected conductor. We went to one of his youth concerts at Garfield High School. It was good.

Over time, things change. Politics! And some of the patrons grew tired of him and attendance dropped. Some of it may have been natural as other forms of entertainment competed for the dollars. "KATIMS RESIGNS!" was the news headline, and I asked him about it.

After Katims retired, I read a story about a concert back East. The conductor wasn't able to continue and a call went out: "Is there a conductor in the house?" Luckily, the Katims were there, and Milton answered the call. He did a great job and got a standing ovation – Faded away? I wonder.

Wesley Fisk was a patient. He was a young member of the Seattle Symphony. Sometimes he'd bring his violin and play a few pieces. It reverberated down the hall, and everyone raved about the beautiful music. I remember he broke his arm and couldn't play for a while. Later he was drafted into the army to serve in Vietnam.

Sgt. Fisk served eleven months as a medic where he had a friend/interpreter named Thin, who had helped keep him alive. Fisk was unexpectedly hurt and airlifted home without a chance to say goodbye and through the years assumed Thin had been killed for helping Americans when the Viet Cong took over in 1975.

Back in Seattle, Wesley had personal problems with drinking and marriage. One day in 2005 while shopping at the Greenlake PCC, he felt a tap on his shoulder. The Asian man asked, "You Fisk?" Wesley, sixty-three, screamed and clutched fifty-eight year-old Thin Binh. Thin had married his girl and gotten to Seattle, working at the PCC. He had no idea where Fisk lived, but recognized the Sargeant's voice. Their renewed friendship helped rehabilitate Fisk.

Richard Fuller, founder in 1933 of SAM, Seattle Art Museum, was a dignified gentleman and supported many local artists like Kenneth Callahan, Mark Tobey, and Morris Graves. With a PhD in geology and a New England fortune, he took no pay until 1973. He and his wife were patients.

I See Dale Chihuly in the building every so often. Once, I told him I did a crown for one of his glass blower workers. I painted a picture of a glass blower's pipe on the tooth. I wonder if he looked. Chihuly dressed like the artist he is – paint all over his clothes and shoes. Big egos make good artists.

Famous Northwest rock sculptor, James Washington, was a patient of Dr. Branch. Once when he came into my office to take a shade, he looked at some of my rock sculptures but didn't say much. He said, "Sam, don't be afraid of changing directions as you carve." Mostly he talked about things like Atlantis and Mu. He was interesting.

Matt Hanford died in 2000. He was just sixty-eight. Heard his family was from Hanford, Washington. I wonder if the atomic project had something to do with his early demise. A lot of "down winders" have had problems. I consider myself a down winder too.

HANFORD NAMED AFTER HANFORD FAMILY?

MY SISTER KIYO & HERB NOJIS SON.

In 1984, my nephew, Rick Noji, stopped by the building right after he was named the top high jumper in the nation while at Franklin High School. He then marked Dr. Branch's office wall at 7' 4½", the height of the record. Rick went on to be a six time All-American at the U of W and is in the Husky Hall of Fame. His best record is 7'7", and at 5'8" tall, he jumps 23" above his own height.

Bob Speyer and Kathy Palmer took us to meet Brian Sternberg. He is also a Husky Hall of Famer with a 16'8" pole vault that was a world record. Brian has been a quadriplegic since 1963 because of a trampoline accident. Kathy is his care taker. Brian does amazing art, holding instruments with his mouth and is a truly inspirational Christian speaker.

SIGNED THE BOOK THE GLORY OF WASHINGTON LIKE THIS!

-PUBLISHED 2001.

Luckily, I know several great artists of the Pacific Northwest. We've bought some original drawings from George Tsutakawa (through our friends, the Maitas), Kenneth Callahan (lived at the apartment managed by Dee's mom, and we visited his Long Beach home), Paul Horiuchi (through cousin Fred Sugita who built the teahouse in the UW Arboretum Japanese Garden), Marvin Herard (neighbors on Capital Hill and long time friends), Manfred Lindenberger (in our building), Aki Sogabe (long-time friend with some of our book projects). Betty Bowen, of the Bowen Award, assistant director at Seattle Art Museum and art critic for the Seattle Times, was a patient and gave me some valuable advice.

As a high school student in Nampa, Idaho, in the fifties, I remember liking this one cartoonist's work in the Seattle Times paper. He created these fake membership cards that ended with "Void if signed by Jack Jarvis". One day, I asked one of Branch's patients, a Mrs. Jarvis, if she knew him. She answered that it was her husband.

"FORTRESS WORLD"

In 1987, Dee's dad had a stroke and went to live with her sister in Los Angeles. Dee gave his car to David Herard, Marv's son. Marv offered a trade of one of his sculptures. We chose the one that went to the 1972 World's Fair in Osaka, Japan, as the Washington State art representation. Marv's mouth contains some of my work as he was a patient of Dr. Reeves.

Dr. Fred Hasegawa and his wife, Kuni, are frequent visitors to the M-DBldg study clubs with Dr. Loomis. Kuni was a spunky young dental hygienist who worked in the building in the sixties. Another aside about the Hasegawas is a popular song of 1964, lyric and music by Paul Weston. Fred's family started that store on Maui, the Hasegawa General Store.

With the Westin Hotel across Westlake Avenue and the Westlake Mall on 5th Avenue, we see a lot of politicians around our building like JFK in a convertible, Geraldine Ferraro, Bill Clinton, John Kerry. Of course, Washington State political candidates are constantly speaking at the mall.

Butterfly guy, Bob Pyle, is a friend and patient of Dr. Branch. Butterfly enthusiasts may be familiar with Bob's books, Butterflies of the Cascadia and Where Bigfoot Walks. He gives David Branch credit for helping and refers to his adventures with "Marsha," his handmade butterfly net; and how it was used, ruined and resurrected. I suggested he make some nets to sell with his books.

Dr. Branch, Dee, and I walked across the street to the Westin Hotel in 1998 and were guests of our daughter, Kelly, who was giving a keynote speech, without notes, for a Thunder Lizard Web seminar. She did well as the audience of seven hundred responded and cheered. Since then, she was part of a small group invited to be guests of Microsoft and to have lunch with Bill Gates in 2008 and 2009.

A STUDENT ONCE ASKED DR BLAND ABOUT VITAMINS. HE SAID, "YOU DON'T NEED EXTRA BUT I'LL RESEARCH IT." HE THEN FOUND LOTS OF DOCUMENTATION PROVING THE NEED FOR EXTRA VITAMINS & MINERALS AND GOT INVOLVED IN NUTRITION.

In the early 1980s, I learned about a nutrition study club in the M-D Bldg organized by Dr. Sondheim and taught by Dr. Jeffrey Bland. Dr. Sab Kajimura got me in and I in turn got Dr. Herb Weisel, his office next door, to join. Dr. Jeff Bland has since that time become nationally known along with Dr. Jonathan Wright, who came regularly and gave a few lectures. Dr. Bland amazed us with his ability to cite peer reviewed articles and dates backing up nutritional alternatives to medical problems without notes.

Learned about Pottinger's cat studies. How they thrived on raw meat versus cooked meat which caused generational sickness. We were introduced to Dr. Weston Price book: Nutrition and Physical Degeneration, containing numerous twenties' and

thirties' studies of pre-industrial populations and comparisons of photographs of teeth and facial structure of traditional diet vs, industrialized foods, with resulting deformities.

Another media person I like is
Robert Schuller. His Hour of Power
is uplifting. Some say he's in it for
the money, but his positive thinking
and stories leave me feeling good;
not like some services that make
me feel guilty. Church should be a
place where one can get recharged.

Working alone, I listen to a
lot of talk radio. I like Rush
Limbaugh's humor and bravado.
He verbalizes things that I only
feel. I enjoy Dennis Prager and
like the way Michael Medved
thinks. Every so often I say,
"Hi", as his office is next door
to mine with Jeremy and Greg.

Since I moved to Room. 854 and
found Medved next door, Dee's
goal is to have him over for
dinner one of these years.

It would be great if teachers,
especially college professors,
taught "How to think", not "What
to think". It also doesn't seem
right that some teachers carry
signs in demonstrations. We can't
help leaning one way or another but
should admit it. I lean right.

Many old timers in Seattle remember the prestige of Gene Clark's Red Carpet Restaurant on the 5th Avenue side of the M-D Bldg. It had an entrance from the lobby of the building. Dr. Sproule often took me to lunch there and naturally, we wore ties. Gene was a patient of Dr. Sproule.

Gene's father, Walter Clark, started his career with little education in 1916. He opened sixty-three restaurants in sixty years. Among them were Around the Clock, The Twin Teepees (did you know that Harlin Sanders perfected his recipe for Kentucky Fried Chicken there?), The Dublin House, The Windjammer and more. His story is in a book Mr. Restaurant.

Here is some of Walter Clark's business creed:

*Always conduct business honestly and ethically.

*Choose partners and counselors who are scrupulous and knowledgeable in their field.

*Employ only the most skilled and dependable person; delegate responsibilities and allow skilled employees to advance.

Fred and Reiko Sugita were patients of
Dr. Branch. Fred, Dee's cousin, was skilled
in Nailless Oriental Carpentry, and rebuilt
the Japanese Tea House in the U of W
Arboretum Japanese Garden. Reiko taught
Japanese Tea Ceremony and was the
Northwest representative to a Kyoto, Japan,
event performed once every one-hundred
years. One of two authentic Seattle tea
houses was an addition to their house on
Beacon Hill. The Seattle Times write up
after Fred's death in 2005, surprised the
Branch Staff because of Fred's constant
joking and self-deprecation. They had no
idea he was famous and skilled.

FRED SUGITA

There are a lot of talented people
in the building. One is Steve Kirk,
a maintenance man. He plays cool
jazz at a local jazz joint several
times a week. He is a good example
of someone pursuing his dream but
being practical with a paying job.

Jerry Schultz is also a gifted
magician. Most dentists are
coordinated and have good hand/
eye technique. Sproule was a good
fly fisherman. A good shot, Hersh
Cox was reported to have been
considered for the Olympic Rifle
Team. A technician of Loomis's
became a full time artist. Dr.
Lindenberger was a well-known
watercolorist. Branch was a college
quarterback.

Because of our kids, we have met some extraordinary people like world famous Dr. Shinichi Suzuki and have learned a lot. Lynette was a precocious child, talked early and walked at eight months. She was a little doll walking under tables. Dee got involved establishing a Suzuki Violin School in Seattle and Lynette started lessons at age three.

Lynette could memorize anything put to music. We didn't expect a musician but understood music, especially violin, could improve right and left brain function.

Dr. Suzuki's philosophy, "Man is a child of his environment," developed when he was a student in Germany and realized all children, no matter their ability learned their native language perfectly as they heard it. He called it the Mother Tongue approach and applied it to learning violin which is considered the most difficult instrument to learn. It increases ability and IQ by coordination of all

the senses. On a couple of his trips to America, we entertained Dr. Suzuki and showed him where I worked in the M-D Bldg on the way to lunch at the Space Needle by Monorail. We also visited his school in Japan in 1971.

Cindi Rinehart, known for her soap opera reviews on KOMO TV, was looking good the last time I saw her. She's the same in person as her vivacious and lively TV personality.

Dr. P. K. Thomas once stopped by Sproule's office. He was famous for the Thomas Technique, Thomas Notch, etc. He had study models of cases he'd done like Eddie Archaro. He told me I had good hands and that Sproule could be a good dentist. Sproule was every bit as good as PK.

Another legendary dentist was Dr. Arne Lauritzen. I'd heard about how he knew occlusion so well. He could fix bad bites and dentures so patients could eat anything. Lauritzen lectured in several languages. He came from a famous family in Denmark and was treated like royalty wherever he spoke. (He was a believer in good nutrition.) Lauritzen was the dentist in "Dennis the Menace" cartoons as Hank Ketchum once lived on Queen Ann Hill.

I was taking a shade on one of Dr. Sproule's patients when the news came over the radio. Elmer Nordstrom was part of the Nordstrom group that bought the Seattle Seahawks in 1976.

This is one of the pages of a leather bound empty book with myThoughts & Stuff. Dee gave it to me for my birthday, January 1994.

"LIFE'S NOT PERFECT
BUT LIFE'S PRETTY GOOD—
LIFE'S PROBABLY TURNING
OUT LIKE IT SHOULD!"
—SG.

One of the first pages in Thoughts & Stuff is this quote from Mary Anne Radmacher that hangs above my lab bench. We got this hand done original in 1990 when we visited her studio in Sandpiper Square at Cannon Beach, Oregon. when she first got started. We've visited her in Salem, Oregon, where she is currently. This and other inspirational work by calligrapher Janet Casey in LaConner, Washington, remind me of the importance of affirmations.

6
Dental Tech World

MY DAD COULDN'T BELIEVE THERE'D BE AN OCCUPATION SUITED JUST FOR ME!

Growing up "disadvantaged" in Bully Creek, my time before, during, and after school I spent exploring rocks, seeing the art in nature, making things with my hands with stuff that was available. I feel these experiences contributed to my work in the dental field. I consider it an advantage that some American schools give students time to do extra curricular projects.

Dental technician work is a worthy profession, but like other skills and handwork industries, modern technology is changing things. Because of the long hours and intensity of the work with constant deadlines, I seldom encouraged young people to consider this profession. I chose this field because other areas of art; and because sign painting, graphics, drawing, and painting wouldn't pay the bills. I decided they were best kept as hobbies. Now, I realize how lucky I have been to make a difference by learning to do my best where I can fill a need. I've benefitted by owning my own business, and it's a good retirement, as I cut back the hours.

Jennings Dental Assistant/Technician School had moved to the M-D Bldg second floor. One day in the seventies, I saw my friend from Quincy, Tom Hirai, through the inside window. Later he said he was checking it out as an investment. He has the ability to check things out before getting too involved. Wish I was like that. Tom is a successful farmer and

LOOKS LIKE TOM, NO IT CAN'T BE!

businessman. He was the first Japanese American to serve on the Federal Reserve Board. Tom came into Seattle every winter from his Quincy farm and earned his degree, one quarter a year, taking eighteen years.

Some basic stuff I've learned about dental technology

On Margins - seal with margin wax 2-3mm on dry, lubed die. Sprue and push off, use the finger-pushing technique.

Invest in a casting ring so the button would be near the center of the ring.

Burn out well - for gold I burn out at least eight hours. Melt the gold with a reducing flame, making sure not to overheat it.

The casting should be black and the sharp edge of the button should not be too sharp. If the gold is overheated, the edge will be knife-edge sharp and especially with gold, the fit compromised.

I scrape contacts two pencil marks (three on last tooth on arch) and check contact with mylar shim strip.

When I first got into dentistry in 1958, things were pretty basic. We used a lot of long pin facings for pontics and baked roots on them. Later, ready-made pontics (Tru-pontics) came out but were more fragile. Long pin facings required putting graphite "leads" into the wax-ups to keep the holes open during burn out. We designed pontics for esthetics or strength, depending on what was more important.

A few years after starting work, porcelain fused to metal came out. It looked better and caused a lot of excitement but had trouble with cracking. The coefficient of expansion wasn't always right. Ceramco, Inc. was the leader in the field and helped a lot with seminars. The early porcelains were air fired but looked good.

BUILDING A ROOT ON A LONG PIN FACING.

IT'S A BIG IMPROVEMENT!

Jelenko came out with a vacuum furnace. We used vacuum pumps from old refrigerators and watched the furnace with one eye while doing something else because we had to cut vacuum 100° below maturity of porcelain. Later, automatics came out. Now there's a lot of excitement with computers, CAD/CAM, and replacing gold with zirconium.

I wondered what he meant. Do most technicians have a bad personality, do I have the kind of personality a good technician should have, or is my personality unusual?

Sometimes it pays to do something poorly. For instance, Dr. Loomis asked me to add some contact to a low fusing porcelain crown. I tried but ended up ruining it. He never asked me to add a contact again.

Dr. David Branch tells how when he was waiting to get into dental school he worked for Loomis. Loomis kept him working as a low paid dental tech. I think it wasn't all bad. It may have helped Branch better understand the dentist/technician relationship because I do work for Branch now.

In the 1960s, dental technicians talked about being more professional with better education, training, and certification (CDT- Certified Dental Technician). Like a degree, it required passing certain tests and required continuing education.

JOE SMITH C.D.T.
• DENTURES
• CROWN & BRIDGE
• ORTHODONTICS
• POP CORN

I studied to take the examination, but it wasn't convenient to take the test. Then I heard of various technicians who had passed sections I knew they weren't proficient in. It didn't seem worth my time and money; but if it were initiated today, I might.

A few years ago dental hygienists wanted to be able to open their own practices, but they couldn't get it passed by the state. However, they could work in nursing homes. Actually, they have it good. They now work when they want and don't have to worry about making appointments, cancellations or business expenses.

--- SO WE COULD HAVE HAD OUR OWN PRACTICES.

(GOOD AT ONE WAY TALK!)

The Thomas brothers had a Dental Laboratory on the fifth floor with three technicians. It was a full service lab with mostly dentures. George was in a wheel chair after a hunting accident so his brother Dick did the leg work. By the time I got to know them, they were talking about retirement.

The lab had a unique look that was artistic in a weird way. The area around the sink was coated with plaster – plaster on the faucets, on the sink bowl, on the walls and on the nearby equipment. Watson Asaba was their "Gold Man." Watson had trained at New York School of Mechanical Dentistry after incarceration of Japanese in Minidoka and was hired by Thomas when the family moved back home. In New York, Eleanor Roosevelt was one of his cases.

Whenever a pretty girl came around, Watson kidded her about sitting on his lap. Like a lot of successful men, he converted his sexual energy into work. He joked about visiting some topless go-go places, but was never unfaithful to his wife. After all, he was an Eagle Scout. He opened his own lab next door so we talked often.

Watson had a Japanese community reputation of being the life of the party, especially with the Rokka Ski Club, where he was an instructor. He continued to be bitter about being incarcerated, taken away in his twenties. The happiest time in his life was when Pauline agreed to marry him and the unhappiest was when he quit going to family events because a relative would get drunk and put him down so bad. Watson's

family was one of the famous businesses in the International District, Sagamiya provided Japanese confectionery food.

Watson retired at age sixty-five when one of his main accounts retired. It may also have been because he wasn't feeling well. At first he did the normal things like fixing up his house and taking up a hobby like horseback-riding. Then he started dropping by my office about twice a week to talk.

One day he stood by my window, telling me things like, "I wish I had taken Pauline to Hawaii and Japan." Two months later I visited him in the hospital. He had had an operation for brain cancer. He never recovered, died in 1987, and was buried in his ski instructor's outfit on a hot day at Washelli. He was sixty-seven.

In the 1980s, we had a crime wave in the building. Watson was robbed of all his gold and needed some in a hurry.

John Smith, a technician, heard about it and stopped by, sincerely offering to help out.

I don't know if Watson ever found out, but John was the robber. He sold Watson back his own gold.

John was turning in extracted teeth that contained gold to a gold dealer somewhere away from the building. A patient of Dr. Branch saw him and recognized him from a picture in the Medical-Dental News Letter. John was put away for the crimes.

There was a technician who did work for government welfare. He would stop by to see Watson, next door, about gold work. Maude Milson did mostly dentures and talked Watson into helping with several cases, but Watson never got paid.

I share this incident because Maude was a charming guy. He is typical of some people, who work for the government, and can't make it on their own. It is often because he can't take responsibility and thinks that everyone else has it better. Free market does a better job of keeping us honest, responsible and always trying to improve, because we can be fired!

After WWII Charles Demming became known for promoting this idea in business.

Gordon King graduated from Jennings School shortly after me and became a orthodontic technician. He could bend wire with the best. He was also a good horse-trader. He liked the excitement of bartering and seldom came out on the short end. He retired and took his mobile home to live in various places. He had never been to the airport. Wonder if he's been to the airport by now?

Bruce Nakamaru, a techician from Hawaii, worked for Dr. Guthrie and then Dr. Brumwell before building a home and lab on Somerset. Being from Hawaii, he was more free and expressive than those of us of Japanese heritage here on the mainland. They refer to us as "Kotonk" (the sound when a mainland Japanese head hits a wall or the floor).

The most decorated 442 RCT unit serving in WWII was made up of Hawaiian/mainland Americans of Japanese heritage. There was a rivalry as Hawaiians thought of Mainlanders as more educated and refined but snobs. The truth is that we envied them, as evidenced by my technician friend, Yosh Fujiwara, who served in the 442nd from the mainland and picked up and continued to use their style of pidgin English.

Bruce told me a ghost story about three boys running through a cemetery with a sack full of fish and all that was left on the other side was a sack full of bones. I submitted the story to a KVI radio Halloween contest and won a Polaroid camera. I gave Bruce a box of chocolates.

Lex Zales worked for Dr. Jim
Amphlet and moved in next door
to me in the 1990s. He was good;
but, working alone and mulling
over thoughts, he got paranoid.
Maybe, it was partly because he
had been a boxer in his youth
and was hit too many times.

Working under a microscope for
hours can put one into a different
world, mentally and physically.
With the stress of perfection
to small details and deadlines, it
leads some people to seek relief
in drinking and other problems.

Somehow, Lex got involved in
suing dentists who wouldn't pay
up. Lex finally had to leave the
building and when he applied for
a job in Texas, he put a couple
doctors as reference. He was
black balled.

One of the colorful characters in the building was Joe Woo. I could hear him as soon as I got off the elevator on the eighth floor where he shared a space with Doug Neal for thirteen years. Joe was not quiet and had nicknames for everyone. Dr. Burtt, didn't have a neck, so he was "The Penguin," Anyone Japanese was a "Raw Fish Eater."

Once, a gal from the blood bank came to their lab to see who was making all the noise. Joe was totally quiet and convinced her it was Doug, who we all know as subdued. When asked to come clean, Joe snickered and whispered: "Laryngitis!"

Joe eventually left our building and the quiet of his being gone left a hole. He went back to school and became a denturist and could work directly on patients. He opened his office in the north end. He died unexpectedly in 2006. At his funeral his daughter told a story of Joe at a karate tournament. To help a Japanese team that was

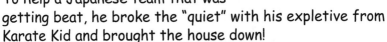

getting beat, he broke the "quiet" with his expletive from Karate Kid and brought the house down!

Doug Neal and I shared work for Dr. Branch. Doug had a commercial fishing boat and went to Alaska every spring so I took over until he got back. It was kind of hard, since I had to find extra work to make ends meet until he went fishing again. On the other hand, I got to know a lot of other dentists, and Doug eventually became a full time fisherman.

Ralph Namba went to Broadway Community College and learned dental tech work under Jim Lincoln. Some stories are hard to tell, but Ralph is a tragic victim of the Vietnam war in my mind. He was deeply misunderstood by family and friends and I gradually learned why. He dropped by often the ten years or so he was in the building and told me his war stories.

In Vietnam he was called "Bambi" because of his ability to run like a deer. He saw new 2nd Lieutenants, who didn't know what they were doing, get killed along with civilians on both sides. He told me stories I can't repeat of women, drugs and war tactics. Ralph was badly wounded both physically and emotionally. His war was indeed Hell. Reading David Bellevia's book of Iraq memoirs, House to House, helps us understand.

Ralph worked for Dr. Loomis until he opened his own lab. Ralph joined a health club and put on forty pounds of muscle (suspiciously fast) and did crazy stuff like let a big hydrocolloid impression sit over a weekend unpoured. He threatened to punch out Loomis when something didn't go right. After his dentist father died, Ralph walked away from his business and never did finish the anterior bridge in his mouth his father had started.

I heard Ralph was jogging on Burke Gilman Trail, and beat up a biker who crowded him off the path. Was wondering about him when Dee was on the same flight to Los Angeles (2009) on his way to a reunion of army buddies. They had a pleasant conversation and he was looking good in retirement.

In 1987, I brought a stereo-microscope. It's been instrumental in prolonging my working life. My cousin, David Nakanishi, helped get it for me. He took over Uncle Ray's Nakanishi Dental Lab and has grown to fifty people. David is a great SOB. Ray is lucky.

Then there was the time I was having trouble taking a shade on a lady because of her bright orange sweater. She offered to take it off. I figured out how to use Blue Brackett Table Covers, which fit around a patient's neck, to block out bright clothes when this happens.

When I see a patient for anterior bridge work, I check the "level" of the face, that the eyes are level, and I note the level of the lower anteriors. Looking at the teeth at an angle can help in taking a shade (it saturates color). Sometimes it helps to squint to better see the value of gray they have.

Ken Barber is a dental tech and author

Doug Wolfe works for Mark Endzell.

A GOOD WAY TO LEARN SAILING!

Tom Enbody was a tech for Dr. Cox. We got together to have coffee a lot. When he got interested in something, he became an expert. He raced prams and won several races using his analytical thinking and some luck in the El Toro, an eight-foot pram with a sail. The shovel on the sail indicated they came out of a bull session.

Dental techs usually have artistic talent, and Tom Cummings is such a person. For a while he got interested in sculpting and did several pretty respectable bronzes. Then he decided to put that ability back into dentistry and studied techniques with some of the best technicians around. He is also an excellent photographer.

AND I'M USING THE LOST WAX TECHNIQUE!

WELCOME TO ツヌトル!

Toyoko Silverman is another talented tech. She worked for the Jankelsons that ran Myotronics and helped with the seminars and was able to speak Japanese to dentists from Japan. She later started Seattle Herbs to go with her dental lab work. She moved her business to her home when rent went up too much. I recently asked her how she liked being home. Her response, "I'm loving it!"

Doug Tsuji stops by the building at times. He worked for Jack Sakai, one of the best technicians in the city. Jack thought highly of him. Doug told me about the pet pig he had for fourteen years in his house. He was told he needed a license for keeping it so he got a vet to come out and give it a physical. The vet overdosed it with tranquilizers and it died. The four pound pig had grown to two hundred pounds by then, was smart, and a great pet.

John Rohan did lab work for Dr. Amphlett, who was most particular, so John had to be pretty good. When he was in the service and in Japan, he met and married Yuko, a little Japanese bride. Back in the states, he realized how young and little she looked when a twelve year old neighbor girl asked if she could come out and play. In some of our discussions we talked about some of the problems we faced in business and in life, and John shared these words of wisdom from his brother-in-law ...

Richard Toida opened a Lab next to me in 424 in 1997. He said, "When the stock market bubble burst in Japan, I lost four million dollars." He was good. He used a mix of Ceramco and Vita procelains with good results. He was just getting established when he developed kidney trouble and had to go back to Japan for treatment.

In the early years, before electronic communication was so good, we used to visit and shop talk about the latest technical things. One day, when I stopped by to see Mark, he was chatting away on his headphone, multi-tasking. I can listen while working but have a hard time talking and concentrating. On the other hand, maybe I get more work done these days.

Several dental techs in the building got involved in a gold mine venture in California (I didn't hear about it). The last I heard was that the government had taken over the property. When questioned, the people behind the venture would always say, "You can have your money back but might miss out."

We techs can be imaginative and somewhat adventurous. One technician bought an old missile silo in Eastern Washington. Not sure what he had in mind, but speculation is that it might be for a survival bunker when things get bad.

Dr. Amphlett, Dr. Helmer & Dr. McAuley

They opened their own dental lab and hired Jim Lincoln. Some of the other techs that were hired were Dale Sperry, John Kanetome and Paul Geroux. Jim went on to head a dental tech school at Seattle Central Community College.

My cousin Yuk then added, "But you don't have to worry about being laid off." (I thought, but we have to keep up with competition, long hours with no overtime pay. On the other hand, it's a life I chose, and Dee was good about it.)

7
MEDICAL-dental Building

The bias of my perspective is that I knew and dealt with fewer physicians.

Older friends, like Tosh and Toshi Okamoto, as well as relatives tell me the Medical-Dental Building was "the place" for their obstetrics and other small medical needs in the 1950s. There is very little history written about the building, perhaps because the residents were busy rebuilding their lives after WWII. Again, I apologize because my views are from the dental related activities.

The existence of a medical hospital in the building and Group Health is evidence of the medical needs served from the beginning until the creation of big medical centers in the 1970s.

In the beginning there were a few more medical doctors than dental doctors. By the 1990s, the directory count lists many more dental specialists than physician specialists. The 2006 directory lists the divisions as Healthcare Specialties and Dental Specialties.

Dr. Fredrick Lemire was ninety-seven years old in 2005. He began his psychology practice in the building in 1937. He served in the navy's 5th General Hospital and was away during WWII. He retired at about ninety-five years of age. His assistant of thirty some years was Grace Friedli.

Dr. Babroff had his dermatology practice near by on the fourth floor. He developed a special formula for beautiful skin and had lots of flight attendants stop by for his product. He had beautiful skin, but was a little overweight. Once, I heard this mocking laughter wafting its way down the hall and a voice saying, "I should lose weight?" One day he was gone, and his formula seems to have gone too.

Dr. Haffley was an eye doctor across the hall from me on the fourth floor for years. He had been a boxer and an army officer. In his seventies he said, "I can't retire because I have an autistic son to support." One day he came across to my office to have me work on his back after he had surgery for boils. I wonder what the patient, waiting in my office entry area, for me to take a shade, thought?

Dr. Homer Harris, a dermatologist, was the first black man in the building. In the 1950s there was still a board of administrators who decided who could practice in the building. There was a lot of discussion before Homer was admitted, but it was proven to be a good choice.

The last time I saw him was, May 14, 2005, when Homer Harris Park on 24th Avenue East was dedicated.

It helped that he was a well known athlete at Garfield High, a college football All-American at University of Iowa before becoming a medical doctor. He also played some as a pro.

It was common to see a line of patients waiting to see him (in the hall). Once, I told him I needed to see him and he said, "Let me look." He looked and said to drop by his office. He gave me some stuff that helped clear it up and refused payment!

He insisted I call him "Homer"; when I'd forget, he'd retort, "Mr. Goto." His mother lived across the street from our house on 23rd Avenue East and he went to Stevens Grade School where our kids went.

My ophthalmologist was Dr. Foxworthy. She had me patch one eye and found I needed a prism. It was too much bother, so I abandoned it. I couldn't help but notice her elaborate jewelry. I heard her marble sized ring was from a dentist friend who even took an impression of her chest area to make a custom necklace for her.

The thirty-three-bed hospital on the third floor was originally on the sixth floor in 1933. In 1988, it had been closed for nine months. Harsch Investment Corp. acquired the the hospital from a group of Seattle physicians in Chapter 11, paid $300,000 delinquent bills and put $500,000 into renovations and Schnitzer opened a $1 million line of credit. Roger Wright, managing director, said, "The facility is the only downtown surgery center." As times changed, Swedish Medical Center and Virginia Mason drew physicians up the hill to Boren and "Hospital Hill."

Late one night, I stopped to talk to the receptionist and tripped on a scatter rug in the entrance of the hospital and found an aluminum teaspoon and a hypodermic needle. It was obviously a set-up for drugs.

In 1990, there was a tragedy. Dr. John Uno, a podiatrist at the other end of fouth floor, died. He was returning from a reunion at Minidoka where Japanese Americans were incarcerated. John's brother and sister-in-law were also killed in the auto wreck near Baker, Oregon. Brothers had married sisters and John's wife, Pat, survived. Tragically, she also died more recently in an unfortunate incident with her son.

Dr. Ted Peterson, also a foot doctor on my end of the fourth floor, made a set of custom arch supports for Dee. At her appointment she showed him the ten year-old lump on her right hand that encased the splinter she had gotten from a shovel handle. He put something on it and in a few days the sliver came out. Such a simple solution to a nagging irritant!

A patient of Dr. Peterson stopped by my office every so often. His name was Hugh Talbot. He was a little man with thick glasses. He was psychic as he passed my doorway on his way to his appointment; he must have sensed that I would listen to him. Once he told me I had healing hands. He showed me how to rub them together to produce energy.

Randy Heine is a receptionist for Dr. M Scott Sr. and Jr., dermatologists. Several of the dental techs used to have coffee with her and one day they made a bet with her. The reader can find out from her why she lost.

My primary physician until his death from cancer was Dr. Norman Arcese. He chose to refuse the routine cancer treatments of chemo and such. I am not sure when he died, but in the 1992-93 directory, he is still listed on the eighth floor. He left the building for a short time and decided he missed the atmosphere here and came back. Someone we came to know because of our Shaklee business, Cory Kempton, once worked for him.

Recently, Dr. Rob Thompson, practicing internal medicine and cardiology on the eleventh floor, gave me a prescription for my Shingles that had closed one eye and extended to my forehead. When the pharmacist gave me the bill it was $140. I said I was surprised. She asked, "You have drug coverage don't you?" I answered, "No!!" So she adjusted it for cash. The new bill was $40. Was I getting charged for the cost of the paperwork at first or what?

For over ten years the Polyclinic has
been on the ninth floor and currently
includes ten primary care physicians, two
rheumatologists, one endocrinologist and
three dermatologists. The original office
where Dr. Poly first began his practice
was on Broadway in a pediatric clinic,
across the street from Swedish Hospital.
The office also included Dr. Robert
Tidwell and Dr. Donald Lewis. Dee worked
there in the sixties.

Once a week Dee accompanied Dr.
Tidwell, in his Chevrolet convertible, to
see patients in his north-end Shoreline
office. That's where she was when
President Kennedy was shot in 1964.

Eventually, Dr. Tidwell
needed some serious dental
work so he became a patient
of Dr. Sproule. They had
known of each other. We
ended up doing a full mouth
restoration on him. It
turned out especially good
as we were able to build his
mouth back to the ideal.
That seldom happened.

Drs. Michael Scott Sr. and Jr. have a dermatology practice on the eighth floor. Michael Sr. became a Who's Who in table tennis but didn't take up the sport until middle age. He was known in the seventies as the most proficient senior player in the Pacific Northwest. He is also a member of the TT Hall of Fame.

MY "ANTIQUE" PENCIL I USUALLY CARRY IN MY POCKET....

THIS ONE WAS FROM MICHELLE WHO BROUGHT IT BACK AS A GIFT FROM JAPAN ABOUT 4 YRS AGO.   11-13-97

ON CLASS - UPPER CLASS, MIDDLE CLASS AND LOWER CLASS. INTERESTING THAT WE ALL SEE THINGS DIFFER- ENTLY BUT --- WHEN AND HOW DO WE BECOME A CERTAIN CLASS?

From Sam's notes on "Thoughts & Stuff"

8
Owning a Small Business

I started my own business at an interesting time when Seattle's bad economic climate was considered newsworthy. I said that if I could make it in the bad times, it was bound to get better. I continued to have my ups and downs but never really bad.

Dr. Gallaher was my first account outside Sproule's office. I remember, in 1969, meeting this tall, dark-haired, charming dentist who had moved into the office on the seventeenth floor vacated by Dr. P. Johnson after he was sent to prison.

Gallaher had a way of helping troubled young people, giving them jobs. Now that he is retired, I miss his lunch room. Dora, his assistant, invited me in for coffee often. We had more time for such things in those days.

> Everyone seems so busy;
> no one stops to chat.
> If I weren't so awfully busy,
> I'd do something about that.

GALLAHER'S LUNCH ROOM

Jan VanderWoude, originally from Spokane, went back to school and became a dental hygienist and continues to work for Dr. Isquith. She talked her sister Barb into coming to Seattle to work for Dr. Gallaher.

After several years of working in Gallaher's office, Barb and Dr. Gallaher married in 1993. They first lived in Laulhurst and then moved to Magnolia where he grew up. Then, Gallaher moved his young, second family to Lake Chelan and commuted for a time. He's now retired but maintains his license, just in case.

I worked with Gallaher for thirty-eight years as he built and retired from a good practice. He sold to Tom McKenny, a young patient (Tom's grandfather was one of the original electricians for our building).

As I cut back my hours to one account, I keep going with a promise to see Dr. Branch to his retirement.

David Branch spent his formative years in Hawaii. In the tenth grade he took a test and scored high in medicine, mechanics, forest ranger, veterinary and dentistry. (I scored high in art, literature and science on a similar test.) Branch says, "As a youth I led a tough and almost delinquent life. I could have gotten expelled when I accidentally punched out a teacher. But I got help from another teacher who tutored me for five dollars. I Couldn't have gotten through school without him."

"Once me and my friend had to hide out from this hood who was set to kill us." Most of Branch's stories are unprintable, and it's amazing he was able to pull himself up to respectability, but as he says, "I've been lucky to have a lot of help from people who believed in me."

In San Diego, he was the top marine recruit in his basic training class. After his stint in the military, he attended Olympic College in Bremerton, commuting on the Kalakala. Then, went to Seattle U on his way the U of W Dental School, graduating in 1973.

Dr. Branch and Heidi working in one of their three operatories.

In 1994 Dianne and Dr. Branch went to Nepal and did some dentistry fo the natives. Their guide, Baboo, was a small man who had come to Seattle to drum up some tourist business.

Kelly gave me the "Gurkha" knife from Nepal. It's well balanced, engraved with birds, and is said to be able to split a skull with a single blow!

The quality of the people in the M-DBldg make it a pleasant place to have a business.

One of the toughest jobs in the dental business is the front desk person. I've seen girls crack-up from the pressure of dealing with people from the office and patients calling and dropping in. The receptionist sets the tone for the business. Luli does a great job for Dr. Branch. She is cool under fire but still friendly, as well as being a private secretary.

Branch's staff keep things fun. They celebrate birthdays, employment anniversaries, and special holidays. Sometimes, patients bring in food, and I'm lucky to enjoy some of the treats. Getting along is challenging, and it is important to keep the welfare and outcome for the patient a priority.

A good example of teamwork is the synergy of Heidi and Dr. Branch as they work efficiently in the mouth. With a grunt or a nod, the right instruments and stuff are there as needed for the procedure.

Always interested in art, Dee and I found the artist, Lynn Dinino, who lived on Capital Hill and made cement chickens that took our fancy. Lynn was able to duplicate them, painted with blackboard paint. We gave one to Branch's office for Christmas and is a fun message board in their reception room.

I did Dr. Reeve's lab work for a number of years when his practice was in the M-DBldg. He opened an office in Des Moines in 1975, eventually, building his own building and closing his M-D Bldg office in May of 2001. I first met Elaine Nakamura, dental hygienist, at an open house for Dr. Ogata's newly remodeled office down the hall from me on the fourth floor; so did Dr. Reeves. Since that time, they are working together and have married. Elaine's good friend is Grace Tazuma, a relative of mine.

In the fall of 1982, Dee tripped on the stairs while bringing products down to the basement. Kelly called me at work. I rushed home, and we took her to Overlake Hospital. She broke her ankle and required surgery, two titanium pins, and an overnight stay. Since then, I've been preaching to women to keep their hands ready to catch the handrails on stairs.

We had planned a trip to Philadelphia and Washington DC. Since we planned to take the week off, we went anyway. At the hotel, Dee slipped on the tile of the bathroom with her crutches and knocked out one anterior tooth and loosened the rest. I replaced the tooth as it was clean. Carrying her to the bed she passed out. Dead weight is amazingly heavy.

I called Dr. Steve Reeves in Seattle in case we needed more dental help than what the hotel gave because he had gone to school at Georgetown U. and I thought he might know a dentist in the area. After we returned home, Dr. Kegel did surgery, Dr. Reeves crushed some bone at root level and we made an eight unit bridge for Dee. It turned out as if we had planned it because Dee had always wanted to get rid of her overbite.

Marshall Frank was one of the last super salesmen. He worked for Jelenko, a national company that sold gold and equipment to the dental profession. Marshall could do it all, and would install, fix, and calibrate dental equipment. I think of him often as an example to follow in taking care of my customers.

HE USED HIS OWN SILVER. AND LEFT NO TRACE OF IT.

When I started my business we saw these sales people regularly. Nowadays, I hardly see any. Maybe it's because I'm so small. They call on the phone, or mostly, I call them. They are just order takers, not much help technically.

Marshall Frank died of a massive heart attack at a dental convention, on the dance floor in 1981. His wife, Betty, called my Uncle Ray (of Nakanishi Dental Lab), the first person she could think of. Their friends and family were his customers. He was loyal to them and they were loyal to him. His company was making some worrisome changes that may have contributed to his early demise.

Bob Shusky was another memorable salesman. He had a limp from having polio as a child.

A Viagra business moved in next door to me for about a year. They were very busy doing mostly mail order. They'd be there late at night like me. I talked to some of the customers and they were pleased with the results. When they moved out, I heard they were bought out for 6 million dollars.

Jerry Erickson had a glass eye business. Unlike us technicians, he was able to work directly on patients. He would take an impression of the eyeball, and then have the patient back for a color match to the other eye, putting in the veins and such. The process is similar to what we do in dentistry.

A Ukrainian man and his two sons opened a denture lab on the eighth floor in the 1990s. They worked hard and even put one of the boys through dental school. I don't know what happened after that, but it was good to see them take advantage of the American system.

In 1978, I tried hiring an assistant. Cal Moss, a technician for Myotronics, suggested I hire Jeanna. She was twenty-five and full of energy. We went to her wedding. I found expenses almost doubled with the cost of her salary with the benefits, social security matching. I let her go when a dentist complained about my quality. It was kind of fun but actually caused more stress and didn't help me reduce my hours.

The American dream,
As you can tell,
Of owning your own business
Is alive and well.

9
medical-DENTAL Building

Dr. Morrison worked out of Dr. Spoule's office, so he was one of the first people I talked with to start this writing/drawing project. We visited him in retirement and, sadly, a short time after his wife had passed away unexpectedly. He explained, "We were recruited to come down and help teach at the new U of W Dental School as it was getting started in the late 1940s. The M-D Bldg was 'the place' so Dr.

GRADUATED FROM TORONTO IN 1943. JOHN'S DADS INFLUENCE GOT ME POSTED TO VANCOUVER. GOT OUT OF ARMY IN '46!

DR. KEN MORRISON CAME TO U.W. IN 1948.

Harrison, Dr. Sproule, and I opened our practices here. We carpooled and I remember having to honk for Sproule, who would come flying out, half dressed with part of his breakfast. We did a lot of sharing as we built our practices. That way the wives could have a car in turns for the kids.

CUTE SOLDIER!

"So you want to know the story of this picture and how I met Marion? I was in Toronto, getting ready for dental school after serving in the Canadian army. I answered an ad for a place to stay. When I knocked, this pretty girl answered ,and I said, 'Well, here I am.' Her mother was renting a room. Later we got engaged. Marion's best friend said she had a picture of me. It turned out the girls had been in Vancouver a couple of years before on a vacation trip. and a sidewalk photographer took their picture. There was an officer in uniform walking by that was in the background of the picture. The officer in uniform was me! Kind of a coincidence?"

Dr. Harrison practiced up the hall from me until his retirement and remembers how he got started and explains, "Dr. Sutcliff was in dental school and suggested I get out of constuction and look into dentistry. I made an appointment with Dean Jones of the U of W Dental School. Jones's first comment was, 'What's with your occlusion?' Not knowing what Jones was talking about, I looked down to see if my fly was open. (XYZ?)" (Harrison has a crossbite.)

Dick Harrison and Stan Sutcliff were talented at drawing and lab work as well as being good dentists. Sutcliff even made a lot of his own cabinets. Once they saw fellow lab tech, Tom Enbody, and me coming down the hall and made the comment about "heavy hitters." It was a nice compliment, but the two of them were the heavy hitters.

Sutcliff was always thinking. Once he thought he'd developed a new porcelain technique. He called it "Flaming", heating it over a bunson burner but it never caught on. He was good about not taking life too serious; during a porcelain seminar by a famous Japanese technician, Sutcliff got the giggles. It was contagious! We all had to hold our breathing to keep from bursting.

Enthusiasm sells! Sutcliff was excited about everything he did. He'd sandblast a crown instead of polishing it and call it a "Florentine finish." He died in 1981 of a heart attack. Days later, Tom Enbody noticed his furnace still on and made the casting of the mold that was burning out. It was perfect.

Harrison's office was up the hall from mine, so we kibitzed a lot. Once he stopped by because he was having trouble with cracking in his porcelain. I couldn't find anything wrong with his techniques or metal design; but I mentioned it was strange that it only

happened on certain shades. That was enough of a clue for him. The new incisal porcelain was the cause. I've learned when an experienced person has problems it's often the material.

THE GROUP OF 9

HANFORD GILBERT McLEAN STARKS HARRISON McPHERSON NOWAK McNILEY MORTON

ALASKA FISH TRIP DENTAL STUDY GROUP 1969

Dr. Harrison is a good cartoonist. This is a sketch of one of Dr. Nowak's famous fishing trips done by Harrison. I traced it and put on some loops to put in the details.

In 1981, Dr. Harrison retired and sold his entire practice to Dr. David Branch. Harrison explained, "I left everything where it was." Later, I got a drawer full of lab supplies and a couple of complete gold teeth. I embedded one in monomer as the liquid started to harden; then it became a clear plastic momento.

Dr. Harrison has a brother named Donn. It turns out he worked with my Uncle Ted Nakanishi in the floor covering business at Schwabachers. Eventually they both went on to be successful on their own. Life is an interesting circle of relationships.

Donn's wife, Ann, worked for Dick as a dental assistant. Their son, David, is an artist. I bought a comp from him. The original is a big mural in the Alderwood Mall, Nordstrom west entrance.

Dr. Lindenberger is well-known for his watercolors. He said, "After doing such intense work like dentistry, I like to be looser with my art." I bought some of his watercolors. I like his example and no matter how much work I put into something, I try for the casual look myself.

Dr. Robert Johnson was an oral surgeon in office 1454, down the hall from Sproule's office but on the inside court. Johnson told me about seeing a heavy object flash by his window (in the 1950s). The object was a man who jumped from the sixteenth floor and died as he hit the third floor roof.

Johnson told me of another time, "I was on the way to coffee on the second floor and saw blood dripping down. I looked up and saw a body on the stairwell screen. He looked pretty dead to me. He was. It was a painter who had been working in the stairwell."

Dr. Johnson retired to his hobbies of hunting, fishing, and playing sax and trumpet. He said in 2005, "I used to be in the Magnolia Band during the big band era. Now I blow some in Chelan and Wenatchee." Music seems to be good for aging gracefully. Maybe next time around, I'll try it. His son, Bob Jr., is now a dentist in the building.

Howard C. Gilbert joined the navy when someone said he'd get drafted into the army. After a three year stint, he came back to the U of W Dental School and graduated in 1952. He joined his dad in the M-D Bldg, down the hall from Sproule on the fourteenth floor.

HARDLY AWAY, I'M HERE IN KIRKLAND AFTER BEING AT PIER 91!

REMEMBER ME?

SHOULD I GO FOR HELP?

One day, an ex-student of Dr. Sproule was "feeling no pain," and was visiting Gilbert. He found out Sproule was down the hall. Sproule had a reputation of being tough on dental students and did things like smear vasoline on a gold foil they were working on. As a joke, Gilbert later sent a "signed" picture from the drunk dentist.

In return, Sproule had me draw a picture of Gilbert in a Batman cowl. Gilbert's assistant/technician, Linda, said, "It looks like him!" Gilbert is well over six feet tall and Linda is hardly five feet. I remember she was from Hawaii and gave me some black coral. She says she saved the picture,

I've been here long enough to see several father-and-son dentists. I've done work for both Arthur Schultz and his son Gerald Schultz. Once, Arthur made castings and had me bake to them, but then the castings changed. They got darker; the fit was okay. I mentioned this to Arthur and it seems he was adding regular gold to his ceramic metal by accident. After he retired, he showed me a wooden eagle he had carved.

Gerry Schultz followed his dad into dentistry and, I think, surpassed him. Gerry is very meticulous. I once said to his assistant, "He seems like a Virgo." He was. Schultz is also a talented magician. He has a lot of stories, and one was about going to the rest room after skiing.

Dr. Jeff Georges' dad was a well known Allergist. I remember seeing family friends from Quincy, where my parents lived, in to see him. His son, unlike his dad became a dentist.

Dr. Frank Endzell was a dentist but his son chose dental technology. With his good hands and analytical mind, Mark could have been a good dentist too.

I only know of one father/daughter dentist team. Dr. Nowak practiced on the fourteenth floor when I was there with Sproule and was known to be quite a fisherman. His daughter Alicia is there now. She also runs a walk-in denture clinic on Olive Way. I've sent several welfare card patients and others her way.

Another father and son was Dr. Al Moore and his son John. Al was a dean at the dental school, worked in the building, and was featured in Time magazine. I remember him saying to his son, "Daddy's got to go potty." Now, John is grown and

has his own orthodontic practice on the eighth floor.

Dr. A. K. Brown moved into the building in 1974 from the Cobb Building. He was commanding officer of his Army Reserve Dental Clinic. I was up in his office one time, and he was reprimanding his assistant for getting bubbles as she was pouring up the models. I pointed out that it looked like trapped air in the original impression material. He thought about it and agreed. Then he apologized to her. It was big of him.

The Takano Brothers were popular orthodontists in our building. Dr. Sproule once said, "Bill was the best student at the dental school." That was until his brother, Jim, came along.

WE BOTH OWN '65 MUSTANGS!

Lou Isquith is a dentist on the sixth floor. He got his assistant, Jan, to go to dental hygiene school. She has been with him for thirty-eight years in 2009.

One day, I got an angry call from Dr. West. He said, "Well, You've got yourself a patient!" A patient of Dr. Sproule's had come to me for advice, and as a technician, we can't work directly with patients. I shot back, "What was I supposed to do? She was a patient of Sproule's, and I'd made the denture!". We got along fine after that. One night around ten at night, several years later, I saw West, loading stuff into his van. We shook hands and said goodbye.

In the 1980s, Linda Leeward was one of the first women dentists in the building. Women were entering the dental profession with good results, especially with children's dentistry. I did some work for her until my workload was too much. I was envious of her safari to Africa where she visited pyramids and saw Lucy, the 3.4 million year-old hominid, which was the oldest then. Now, Ardi goes back 1 million years before.

On one of my breaks, I was looking at some pictures of famous art in Life magazine. I noticed a picture of a cross-eyed lady. I read more and found out it was owned by a Dr. Saul Schluger, who was a friend of Dr. Sproule and came into the office quite often.

Dr. Schluger was a well-known instructor of periodontics at the U of W Dental School, and a collector of art. Among other things, he was a good example of the old addage, "Those that can, do; and those that can't, teach." He knew how but his big hands couldn't.

We've had patients with very protrusive anteriors (bucked teeth). Extractions and bridges have made big differences.

Dr. Yosh Ogata was an orthodontist on the fourth floor. I liked his thinking of no mouth breathing, tilting teeth instead of extracting, and how the tongue affects occlusion. He lectured and had a good reputation. He also had some detractors. It seems for every new idea, there's someone that differs. It keeps things interesting and grows the profession.

Dr. Jadine Acena had her office in 1435 but retired (still young). Jadine's brother is married to my cousin Sharon Nakanishi. Jadine sold her practice to Dr. Jim Cherberg on the tenth floor. I asked Cherberg about his familiar name and he said, "Dad, John, was lieutenant governor of Washington State for thirty-two years."

Dr. Bernard Jankelson was quite a dentist. Some called him a charlatan. He invented a battery powered muscle stimulator. He called it the Myomonitor. It was designed to open and close the mouth and relax facial muscles. I was intrigued because dentists were coming from all over the world to his seminars. I've heard geniuses are unappreciated in their home towns so I signed up to take a course.

A denture patient with a long history of TMJ (temporomandibular jaw joint) problems was helped a lot during the seminar. Dr. Jankelson was a good talker and salesman. Some of his ideas were no deflecting cusps, muscle memory creating propreoception (biofeedback), and muscle is stronger than bone.

After taking the course, I was asked to do some full mouth cases for a dentist who had taken the seminar using the Myomonitor. Although some cases had good results, I found it disappointing because we could never get a good centric. The cases turned out okay because I'd had experience with big cases working for Dr. Sproule.

Andrew Shields was a good dentist, liked by everyone and had a good practice. But it was considered strange in the seventies and eighties that he took a partner and they both wore tight pants. They were always willing to share and talk about the latest dental information with us techs.

They eventually got a "divorce" and both died of AIDS. Some patients complained about not being told, but they were very careful and particular about their techniques.

HANDLE WITH CARE!

I THINK IT'S PAST LIVES!

SOME SAY ITS GENETIC. SOME SAY IT'S LEARNED.

Since then, I've heard a doctor say, "Sperm is not a foreign body to females, but to males it is and stresses their immune systems over time." If true, a vasectomy might help prevent AIDS. There is no definitive conclusion why people are gay, but I'm sad for them.

Dr. Herbert Fleege and Dr. Pat Fleege became well-known children's dentists, partly because they had monkeys. The younger Pat Fleege's monkey got so attached and was jealous of his wife.

My nephew, the high-jumper, had a Filipino friend who wanted to keep his tradition of feeding a monkey on New Years Day, so I got them in touch with Fleege.

The younger Fleege met a young lady dentist in the hallway. She was Stephanie Marvin (I wonder if the monkey was involved?). Now they are married.

After a divorce, Dr. Fleege Sr. decided to move to Mexico. He bought a Salvation Army truck, loaded it with stuff. When he was stopped at the boarder, he showed them the back of the truck filled with religious artifacts and was told to go on through.

Dr. Paul Genung is a white-haired dentist who believes in health-conscious dentistry. He believes like Dr. Huggins that mercury is a problem in dentistry. He pointed out to me that dentists used to have the highest rate of depression and suicide of any profession. He said, "Mercury is a neuro toxin and is not allowed in Europe."

Dr. Simpson retired at age seventy-five in 2007 but came into my lab for a shade check. While working on his case, he shared some interesting stories. He said, "I remember Dr. Newfield calling me at home and going on and on about what a good person I was. On a hunch, I decided to go back to my office...

...and found Newfield in a chair enjoying the results of nitrous oxide. He was no longer allowed to have his own office and had climbed in through a window. He used to be on the sixteenth floor, where I had my office, and he knew how to get in through the patio."

Another Simpson story was about this handsome dentist who liked the girls and was taking money out of the till for "continuing education" with his secretary. This dentist was known for his loud voice. Once, he'd given a well-endowed patient a shot to numb her mouth, but he couldn't get his mind off her breasts. When he came back to see if the anesthetic had taken effect, he said in a loud voice, "Are your tits numb yet?"

Olin Loomis was an exceptional dentist and had quite a following. He was the mentor of a well-known study club in the building. Being on the same floor as Sproule and doing similar work, we were friendly rivals. He always chided me on retruded centric.' Dr. Sproule liked to start with retruded centric but always ended up with long centric. Once in front of a patient, Loomis said, "Sam, you hate my guts don't you?" I said, "Yes, but I respect you anyway!"

"After Cheryl read my figures wrong & under paid me. I learned to write better."

It was a great course. I gave Loomis a gift certificate to Nikko Restaurant in return. Able came to Loomis's funeral in 2006 and left flowers on a memorial poster in the M-D Bldg. lobby. Loomis had played golf a few weeks before.

One day in 1987, I took a shade on a patient of Dr. Brown, who was a chaplin at Swedish Hospital. The next day, I attended the funeral of a friend, Jim Mitchell, and the patient was the minister in charge. I said a few words about how Jim was always making plans. Gary Green mentioned how Jim was constantly trying to live one more day. (He died of cancer.)

Dr. Teller was next door to me
on the fourth floor for years.
One day in 1973 a neighbor,
Sumi Akizuki, dropped by our
new house on Mercer Island
with her friend, Aiko Goshi. I
had known Aiko in Bully Creek,
Oregon. Her younger brother,
Jim, and I were friends in the
forties. As we visited, I learned
that Aiko was a house-keeper
for Dr. Teller in Issaquah.

Dr. Jim Voget taught me about
keeping the tops of contacts level.
I did some work for him when
Diana worked for him. He is a good
analytical thinker so I was surprised
when he had a bad bicycle accident
that put him in the hospital.

I heard Dr. Roger Harper
on a radio talk show
once. He was interviewed
about dentistry and very
knowledgeable. He also has
a great radio voice.

Dr. Ron Bryant bought Dr. Spoule's practice in 1981 and thirty years later still has his original crew; Casey, Kathy and Sharon. It says a lot about the quality person he is.

Dr. Wally Kegel's periodontic office on the sixth floor is like going to a photo gallery with his collection of antique cameras and his pictures of animals from Africa. It's because of his work that Dee's bridge turned out so good. I've also had work done by him.

Dr. Frank Baird was a good friend of Dr. Sproule, practicing next door until moving to Wenatchee. Frank's son David, while in dental school, often dropped by my office at night to learn more about lab work. One night he brought a young lady, his new wife. Since then, David has become a well-known lecturer, on bonded porcelain and esthetics, world wide. He invited me to one of his lectures at the Museum of History and Industry. Another time, he invited me to a precision casting course in Wenatchee.

In 2004, the Washington Dental Service (WDS) celebrated its fiftieth anniversary. The M-D Bldg was the birthplace of this group and now includes Delta Dental Services. Longshoremen and warehousemen unions decided to fund prepaid dental care for member's kids with surplus money they had...

...I remember the controversy. It caused talk of 'Capitation' – setting the price member dentists could charge and socialized dentistry. "It doesn't make dentists better, just makes bad dentists worse." OSHA regulations increase prices. But private co-ops were catching on.

Dr. David Branch was second chairman of WDS, 2009, and stopped by to introduce me to the President, Ron Inge.

In the early years, dentists washed their hands and, of course, brushed their teeth and used breath fresheners. Now, they have added requirements like gloves, long sleeved shirts and masks. OSHA regulations include Back Flow Valves, Sink Traps, special soiled item bags, etcetera, etcetera.

We visited the Amphletts in their Mercer Island home. Jim was getting ready to go on a fishing trip up north and was making some fishing lures. I enjoyed their "Pig Farm" picture.

Dr. Joe Zimmer has now expanded to take in the entire seventeenth floor. I remember when he was just starting his rooftop garden. We both went out to a nursery in Magnolia and bought some bonsai from China and out of quarantine. All of mine died, and I think all of his died too. His roof garden has been in several magazine articles and getting to be well-known.

10
Out My Fourth Floor Window

When first coming to the M-D Bldg in 1958, women had big hair and long skirts. Amazing how fashions change. Some economists say skirt length is tied to the market. When skirts go up so goes the market and vice versa.

The reasoning is that people get more daring, so skirts go up. People are more optimistic investing, and taking more chances, pushing the stocks up. With women wearing pants, it's hard to tell where stocks are headed.

Or? With women wearing pants, maybe I should consider the "boob effect"; the more cleavage the better the market. Looking out my fourth floor window, I have a good view and it looks encouraging. On the other hand, maybe it will take a lot more observation and research.

I must admit, I can't tell lies;
Looking out my window just rests my eyes.

I had problems with installation of my air conditioner on the fourth floor (air intake and exhaust were reversed). I couldn't get the upper sash down when a window washer came in the door. He offered to help. He stepped out the window, no straps. I couldn't watch. This was the fourth floor. He balanced and banged on the upper window and got it loose. Scared the H___ out of me!

In the 1970s, there was a guy who called himself Conan. I'd see him peddle by with his big broad sword on his back. He was a good guy and was actually credited with breaking up a crime on First Avenue.

In 1986 the Westlake Center building was built. The monorail track was changed and curved so it would line up with the terminal on the third floor of the center. The curve created a pinch point where it wasn't possible for two trains to pass without sideswiping. Someone forgot and the accident shut down the monorail and hurt businesses for a year or so.

Catastrophic weather changes
are a normal part of planet Earth.
40m yrs. ago Mt. Rainier started
to form, 15m yrs. ago basalt lava
covered the Columbia Basin, 18,000
yrs. ago Seattle was under 4000 ft.
of ice. 15,000 yrs. ago the Missoula
floods created the present Eastern
Washington landscape. Are global
changes influenced by man? Maybe
the warming we are supposedly
creating has delayed another ice age? May of 1980, Mt. St.
Helens blew its top reminding us of nature's fury.

The winter of 1981-82 was cold!
A cold front from Canada iced
the roads and sidewalks for
most of November. I particularly
remember that year because I
lost some bonsais to the cold.

The winter of '82-'83, I was snowbound!
I had a great view from my fourth floor
window of the whipping snowflakes and
drifts. I decided to stay and sleep on the
floor. A lot of people who worked downtown
stayed in hotels. I had heat and electricity
so it wasn't too bad. Besides, it gave me a
chance to get caught up on my work.

I talked to Dee, and she couldn't get
home either, spending the night at
Mercer Island Denny's and in the car
with a neighbor. It was just as well, as
there was no electricity at home for
several days.

In January 1993, we had some bad windstorms. Dr. Gallaher, on the seventeenth floor, had a window blow in from the 70-mph wind (over this is hurricane force). He protected his patient with his body, but she was cut on a leg. It took four people to put plywood over the blown out window.

Once, during a windstorm, the window of Sproule's office blew open, and the glass popped out. I watched as it fell fourteen floors and prayed it wouldn't hit anyone. It crashed harmlessly in the intersection of 6th Avenue and Olive Streets.

A construction man was working on the roof of the Westin Hotel and tried to hold down the plywood. He was blown away and carried to his death from the fifth floor level!

In march of 1983, Queen Elizabeth visited Seattle. She walked from the Westin Hotel on a red carpet that was roped off with security all around. Meanwhile, a girl on the eighth floor of the M-D Bldg exposed herself to the guards: "Just testing the alertness of the guards!"

Eighth floor of M-D Bldg

Dr. Branch works hard, but he also likes to have fun. For Luli's fortieth birthday party he had a male stripper in for a surprise.

HAPPY BIRTHDAY!

DR. BRANCH, OUR PATIENT MRS. SMITH DIED—IT'S HER, SAME NAME AND MIDDLE INITIAL!

THIS IS MRS. SMITH—YOU SAID I NEEDED A FILLING BUT NEVER CALLED ME!

WHERE ARE YOU CALLING FROM? IS IT HOT THERE?

...... A SHORT TIME LATER THE PATIENT CALLED!

Taking a noon walk to the Westlake Center, I saw a naked man walking on 5th Avenue and Olive Street. I ran back to get my camera, but it was too late. He seemed in a daze; I never heard any more about it.

One December in the 1980s I looked out my fourth floor window and saw this nude guy with a towel around his neck on the fifth floor of the Westin Hotel across the way. He must have been proud of his manhood because every so often he reached down and tugged. Working late, I saw others who forgot to pull their shades.

A building maintenance man told me of being called to help a naked lady in the hall of the twelfth floor. Apparently a tenant entering the restroom found a street person stripped and washing up. She was told to get out and she did.

One summer day in 1999, I thought I
heard a shot! Looking out my fourth floor
window on to Westlake and Olive way.
A guy was slowly walking away from an
orange taxi cab, leaving a trail of blood.
There was also a big puddle of blood near
the cab, stopped at the light.

As I watched, the man
stagger away towards
Stewart Street and the
Westin Hotel, There were
more shots. The cab driver,
wearing a white coat and
a big white turban, kept
shooting. Then, he calmly
got into his cab and drove
up Olive Way. The wounded
man fell at the crosswalk
near Stewart.

A young man rushed over to the
intersection and tried to stop the
bleeding with his t-shirt, but the
man died. It was a territorial feud.
Months later, I got a call from
Sam Chapin who was a neighbor
of ours on Mercer Island and a
classmate of our daughter, Kelly.
He was with the prosecutor's
office, and wanted me to be a
witness. I even got a subpoena.

Every so often a seagull stopped by my window. It was fun to throw food to them and watch them dive and catch it in full flight. The building asked us, "Please don't feed the seagulls, It will attract more."

Bums are known to never go hungry in Seattle and there is almost always one in front of Bartell's on the Fifth Avenue side of the building. I used to be an easy target. I was told stories like, "I need twenty dollars to get back to Vancouver. I'll pay you back with interest." One time, instead of giving money for food as he asked, I told him I would accompany him to the café. He actually wanted money for his alcohol problem; most are on drugs or are mentally ill, and many should be institutionalized.

So what's the difference from the bums and the birds? More will come. I heard San Francisco spends twenty-four thousand dollars a year per bum (2002).

Conditions were right for an earthquake. I had my camera ready. The moon was in perigee and the atmospheric pressure was high. The quake hit at 10:54 a.m. on February 28, 2001. I grabbed my camera, braced myself, and took pictures of the swaying flag poles and the surrounding plants. The developed pictures were disappointing. The pictures come out looking normal because they are still pictures. Maybe it's my imagination, but there is a bright sparkly look.

The speaker system in the building ordered us to get out, but I stayed in the office until someone of authority came by and told me to get out. We all gathered across the street on Olive Way. Dr. Branch was there in his Ford Explorer and suggested we take a ride. We saw damaged buildings, bricks on cars, and some sidewalks messed up.

At our West Seattle rental house, Dee had just left after two men delivering a new washing machine had walked under the brick chimney that collapsed. Luckily, all the bricks fell in the yard between our house and neighbor's house. I had to fix one broken pipe. We had about ten thousand dollars worth of damage. The insurance didn't cover earthquakes. Government FEMA wouldn't help on a commercial building.

AS SEEN BY A LADY ACROSS THE STREET.

As seen by lady across the street.

PIGS ON PARADE - FIBER GLASS
PIGS DECORATED BY LOCAL ARTISTS.
ABOUT 200 SCATTERED AROUND
DOWNTOWN SEATTLE THIS
SUMMER.

THIS BEACH ONE IS ONE
OF MY FAVORITES - IN FACT ITS
WHAT I'D HAVE DONE, - THOUGHT
OF IT BEFORE I SAW IT.

"CREATIVITY IS MOSTLY
PROBLEM SOLVING - "
SC.
6-18-2001

A page from Thoughts & Stuff. Summer 2001, Seattle created the first Pigs on Parade. In 2007, Seattle celebrated the 100th Anniversary of the Pike Place Market with a second pig art event. They sponsored a contest for the most creative Pig because the original pig was the one at the market. There were pigs on every street corner throughout the downtown sector of the city. It was fun.

We all have some unusual people in our lives. Fred is such a person. He comes in every fall and just hangs around. He is a nice person but sort of lost. Dr. Branch's friend Richard, from Australia, does the same. He gave me a small gold nugget he found. But, I remember him most for his photo of "Paradise" taken near Lake Wenatchee. I remember it had a guy, a gal, a dog, sun, and water.

11
Interesting?

Still working at the lab bench built in 1969 when I opened my own lab.

STUFF UNDER THE CLOCK: An original Disney (my first hero) cartoon strip from Kelly and an original hand written quote that says "Dare to Believe In Your Own Creativity" by Mary Anne Radmacher. I am inspired by original works of artists on my walls, and committed to meeting all the artists in person.

ON THE FILE CABINET: A piece of pottery by Hiroshi Ogawa from Elkton, Oregon. The photos are of our five grandkids.

ON THE BENCH: An 8-ball from my army days. I use it for a bur block. It is a reminder of the wastefulness of government. We had to dispose of many things and use up the budgeted money to justify our yearly quota or we would lose it for the next year.

When I first came to Seattle in 1958, I stayed with my sister Kiyo on fifteenth Avenue, between Fir & Spruce. I owe her a lot! I was too broke to contribute much for a year. Rent was about fifty dollars a month. She had come to Seattle earlier to go to secretarial school and worked as a housekeeper for a family in Laurelhurst. She had been on the honor roll in high school and was Nampa High Lettuce Bowl queen in 1952. She was working for Milliman & Robertson, an actuarial consulting firm, started in 1947 and now has fifty-two offices around the world.

I was enrolled in the dental tech school downtown, and one morning while waiting for a bus on Jefferson street, a young guy rushed up, pounded up a poster and said, "Vote for Sam Smith!" I said, "Who's that?" He said, "That's me!" He impressed me as being ambitious, and I voted for him all the time after that. He's become famous.

One day, Kiyo asked me to draw a picture of a group of people at a board meeting. I just guessed as to how they would look. The card turned out uncannily like a photo taken earlier. They had me redraw it for framing. I think Kiyo transmitted it to me psychically. My mom was like that too.

Kelly was three years old when she started dialing and calling me at the office when she wanted to talk. She was eager to start first grade but then started to complain and was even sent to the principal's office. We didn't understand ...

... until we attended an open house. We met her teacher, and she thought Kelly had too big an ego. I recalled my own first grade experience when I wouldn't play with the girls. My teacher broke my spirit and forced me. I didn't want this to happen to Kelly so we changed schools.

Kelly did well after that and scored so high on a couple tests she was put in an advanced class. (Lynette had skipped a grade so Kelly was pleased.) Her third and fourth grade teacher was Mrs. H. Davis, a gifted teacher who helped bring out the best in Kelly in those

important years. She understood troublemaking kids could actually be bright.

According to Bobb Biehl, age nine might be the most important age in life. He says the brain starts to specialize around then, so who you are at that age is the core of who you are as an adult. So it seems important to expose kids to a lot of different things before age nine. The expression, "His art is stuck in the third grade," has some validity.

In the seventies, Sam Takahashi worked for MarikoTada, a Japanese antique store on the street level of the M-D Bldg. I bought a few things like a 'Goto' Kozuka (small utility knife, accessory to a Samurai sword), and a nineteenth century Japanese dish repaired with gold. I remember him most because he asked, "Would you come to my wedding?" instead of "could." It was a beautiful outdoor wedding in West Seattle.

SAM, WOULD YOU COME TO MY WEDDING?

FOO DOG DISH

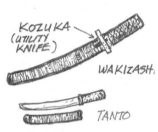

KOZUKA (UTILITY KNIFE)

WAKIZASHI

TANTO

About that same time, a patient brought down two Japanese swords to sell me for $175. That was a lot, but I agreed after taking them apart and checking them. I thought we had a deal. Shortly, he came back, out of breath. I'm sure he had stopped at the antique store. I was disappointed, but it may be just as well because owning too many swords becomes a worry.

Earlier, I mentioned the famous dentist Dr. Arne Lauritzen. Son, Arne, was a patient; I think he still has some inlays we made for him in the sixties. Young Arne had a paper route, and one of his customers had a Japanese sword. Arne admired it and was told he could have it someday. He forgot all about it, but years later a lawyer delivered the sword to him because the customer had left it to Arne in his will. Then in the 1990s, Arne gave me the sword. It seems the customer had gotten the sword during WWII and Arne decided it belonged back in the hands of someone whose culture was Japanese.

SAM, THOUGHT YOU SHOULD HAVE IT!

Charlene Strong, dental assistant and interior designer, in the building, lost her partner, Kate Fleming, who drowned during a Seattle historic, bad rainstorm flood in 2004. Kate had gone to her basement to recover her "Voice Over" business equipment and was trapped. Only family was allowed in the hospital and able to make funeral arrangements. Despite her grief, Charlene worked to tell her story and legislation was later passed to allow family rights for domestic partners.

I met another Dr. John Sproule in 1995 aboard a Japanese training ship from Hokkaido. We were guests of Joe and Mariko Maita. Joe was a graduate of the well-known maritime school and was part of the reunion in Seattle. Not sure why this Sproule was on the ship, but his physique and mannerisms were eerily similar to the Sproule I knew. He must be related.

Remember the ubiquitous phone booths? Hard to find these days. Superman would have quite a problem!

When I moved to the eighth floor, I decided to go with the cell phone only.

I used to park where the new police station is now. Across the street to the south was a three story building that had evening art classes featuring live nudes. So when I worked late, I saw the end of the class. The nude model put on her robe and looked at the art students' work. It gave me an incentive to get out by 10 p.m.

One night walking up Olive Street, I passed a policeman standing at parade rest in the alley between 6th Avenue and 7th Avenue. I stopped to look. There in the alley beneath the fire escape stairs was a young man lying on his back, dead! The cop said, "He either fell or jumped."

Another late night, I ran across a darkened street and tripped on the edge of work being done to resurface the asphalt. I could have fallen on my face but remembered my Aikido and thought, "roll." It saved getting hurt.

The Mariners Baseball team won 116 games to tie the Major League record in 2001. Isn't it interesting that the mirror image of 116 is 911? It was also the year Ichiro became the first position player from Japan as well as becoming an All Star.

The 6.8 Nisqually Earthquake on February 28, 2001, caused a lot of damage, but no one was killed. In September, Dee made plans to attend a book-signing party in San Francisco for Kelly's book that had hit the top of the Amazon ratings. We were up early and saw the first tower hit but left for the airport before we understood the gravity of the 9/11 terrorist attacks. I couldn't get back to the airport to pick Dee up again. She says, "I was part of a mass migration of pilots, flight attendants, and passengers walking with their roll-on bags heading for the International Boulevard." I picked her up when she called. It was before we carried cell phones.

Noting coincidences: one of our best friends, Anna Uchikura, has her birthday is on February 28th (same day as Seattle's Nisqually earthquake that year) and her sister, Azusa, has her birthday is on September 11.

Dr. Sproule had a patient and friend, Frederick. It was interesting because his teeth and bite conformed to his constant clenching of a pipe. In other words, he could touch his teeth together with his pipe in place.

The building had a security guard that began his evening about five o'clock and stayed all night. We had to sign in if we came in after six. We still had quite a bit of crime. Thieves looked for open offices.

My office in 423 was broken into twice. Some sort of thin wedge opened the locked door and a small pry bar was used to get cabinet drawers open. I had a cop dust for fingerprints but found none. The thieves were looking for drugs and overlooked some silver coins I had. Later the building installed deadbolt locks free.

A favorite way to get in was to come into the building before 6 p.m. and stay in one of the rest rooms until everyone went home. After installation of surveillance cameras, a guard recognized one of the suspects and called the cops. I witnessed the arrest (1991) as I was working late. It seems two were working as a team because a girl was also involved.

Carl, a maintenance man in the building once told me, "I kept my lottery tickets for a year and in January it was over three hundred dollars. In the late sixties, the lottery was supposed to eliminate school levy votes. It hasn't helped. It all goes to the general fund and is used by the government. I don't like the idea the lottery gives people about getting rich by luck and not work.

I keep a cup on my desk commemorating the 1978-79 World Baskeball Champion Seattle Super Sonics. It was an exciting time. D.J. was the star and spark. I remember going home late that night in June. Fans were celebrating in the streets. Actually, things got out of hand; they turned cars over. Now it's sad to look back and see that a goal to just win a championship is not enough. The team splits up and the good players are gone.

I have a metal sculpture in my office done by a patient. We had done an eight unit bridge for him, and I charged him only for the gold. David Dawson asked me what I'd like. I said, "Maybe a family tree." I had seen pictures of his work. The picture looked small but it turned out to be about three feet tall. It is hollow metal, welded and painted to look like wood. The Goto and Miyamoto family crests are at the bottom. Nice!

IN 1889 FROM GLENNS FERRY FOR-MATION - NAMPA IMAGE COULD BE 2 MILLION YEARS OLD

READING & LISTENING TO TAPES AT WORK.

I enjoy theories about early man. Forbidden Archeology by Michael Cremo is good - even when he spells Archaeology differently. I realize we're only blips in the scheme of life. It puts things into perspective, like money need not be the measure of success, but at least earn enough to be generous.

In 1995, Dee arranged for a surprise trip to Hot Springs, South Dakota. We visited the mammoth site built by Larry Agenbroad, a high school classmate from Nampa High. We dug for bones with Earth Watch members and found some twenty-five thousand year-old fossils. Larry was class president and I was vice, but Larry's wife, Wanda, outranked us. She was student body secretary.

LARRY, YOU HAVEN'T CHANGED MUCH SINCE HIGH SCHOOL!

DENTAL TOOLS FROM BRANCH

DR. A.

EXTINCT WITCH HAZEL EOCENE 50 M.Y.O.

Someone in the building mentioned going up to Republic, Washington, to find fifty million year-old fossils at Stone Rose site. Dee and I drove up one weekend in 2002, past Coulee Dam and almost to Canada. The dig was a hill that was once a lake bottom. I split a big slab and found a beautiful leaf that I have framed. In the fall of 2009, we visited again with Heidi and Larry. We learned Ranald MacDonald was buried near by. He is credited with being the first teacher of English in Japan in 1848 and his students interpreted when Commodore Perry opened isolated Japan to world trade in 1853.

To do research for this book, we visited Dr. Harrison and Patty at their Bainbridge Island home in 2004. Their house looks toward the southern tip of Widbey Island and Edmonds. It is built on a spit shared with a few other houses, a beautiful place.

Dee and I visited Harrison because we had stayed near by in a traditional Japanese style inn (Ryokan), built by Ron Konzak on Love Road. We had known Konzak from our old neighborhood on Capital Hill as he was part of the group that made The Gooey Duck Song popular in the sixties. It turned out that Harrison considered the song one of his favorites and played it for us.

In the 1960s there was a band in Seattle called the Pierymplezaks. The name was the combination of Paul Pierce, who lived across the street from us on 23rd Avenue East, Bob Dalrymple and Ron Konzak. They practiced at the Pierce home. Ron wrote the song and even sang part of it in Japanese.

OSIE VERGEN

HEIDI MASSUKO

"FLIRTING IS THE ART OF MAKING ONE FEEL GOOD!"

LULI WEATHERWAX

BUSTER KANETOMI

DR. STEVE REEVES

SCOT CHRISTENSEN

I was born in Seattle during the heart of the Great Depression and constantly reminded of it.

I hear history repeats every seventy-five years or so. It takes about that long to forget past history.

We lived in shacks with no electricity, no running water and an outside privey in Bully Creek, Oregon.

Walked to a one-room school three miles in all kinds of weather.

Moved almost every year because of WWII. I was called names because of the war but thought life was like that. When you're young everything seems normal

Worked in fields for about a dollar an hour. It was fun in work crews. Money went to help with family expenses. Farming was the only life I knew.

School friends were white; weekends were with friends like myself

Got a raise to four hundred dollars a month when I married but wasn't allowed to live in certain districts in Seattle

12
Building and Creating

It's interesting to watch businesses on the street level of the M-D Bldg. They thrive and grow, quit, go broke I've seen cigars, restaurants, pharmacy, glasses, antiques, jewelry, men's clothing, women's clothing, picture framing, vitamins, ice creamery, cell phones. One thing I've noticed; people are like bugs, and are attracted to light. I'm lucky, I've been here to see most of those small businesses come and go.

THE TOOTH COUNTER –DRAWERS OF DENTURE TEETH & PONTICS.

Arnold Dental Supply moved in after Patterson moved out. It was handy to have them in the building. Now, it's mostly mail order. I remember Mark, the repairman, Steve West and Darrel and Doris with the look of the seventies with long hair, side burns, and polyester bell bottoms. Dress got real casual. Before that time we wore ties and sport coats.

The original builder of the M-D Bldg, Metropolitan Building Corporation, sold to Harsh Investment Corporation on February 1, 1977. Former Manager, Bob Burton was retained for a while. Later Chuck Karl took over. Chuck Karl was a Vice President of Harsh Investment Corporation and managed the building until his retirement in 1986.

Harsh Investment Corporation is a Portland-based real estate management firm, headed by Harold Schnitzer, with extensive holdings in the West. Harsh later sold to Goodman Real Estate in August 2005 for thirty-eight million dollars. Goodman put eighteen million dollars into remodeling, and it was put on the National Registry of Historic Places for which they got tax credits. (Thanks to writer Mildred Andrews for her help.)

When the building was new with the second addition in the 1950s, the lobby included the space between the elevators with a double set of doors for protection from harsh weather as we entered. The floors were terrazo and the walls and trim around the elevators were beige marble. The ceiling was vaulted, later lowered. Today, it's vaulted again. The marble was covered for a while, now exposed again.

We had elevator girls in uniforms operating each car and they asked: "What floor please?" When the car was full the starter "clacked" hand held castanets, held out an arm, and closed the door. They knew all the tenants and room numbers.

After hours (evenings and weekends), we pressed a button to call for an elevator. One person was on duty and answered the bell by going to the lobby or floor that called. Some impatient people rang constantly, thinking it might speed up the operator. It only made him mad.

In 1958, the building was a prestigious place. Everyone dressed up to come downtown.

The Red Carpet Cafe on the second floor was a branch of the Red Carpet Restaurant on the street level. It was a premier restaurant with great food. The soup was made downstairs and sent up. In the cafe, they had special seating sections for doctors and even a small smoke shop. Men even put on ties to come to lunch there.

I usually sat with the other technicians and assistants, but some times I'd have coffee with the doctors. It was a fun meeting place, full of energy and optimism. It was a place to catch up on the latest gossip and the latest jokes. Things change. Before I knew it, an era went by and that time became the good 'ol days. It's time for the next generation.

Some of us remember the men's store on 5th Avenue, now Bartell Drugs. One of the salesmen there was very overweight by 1960 standards. Stomach stapling was fairly new, but he wanted to give it a try. He died from complications.

PRE-WESTLAKE CENTER

Ben Paris was a well-known sports restaurant in the sixties before the mall was built. Once, I tried to treat Dr. Sproule & Shirley to lunch at the new Space Needle, but Dr. Sproule caused us to miss our reservation and we had to take the monorail back to Westlake Station. We had lunch at Ben Paris. Anyway, it didn't cost as much.

Coming into the lobby in the early years, on the right was Western Optical, on the left was Kelley-Ross Pharmacy. Beyond the elevators was an entrance, with a half flight of stairs, to the Frederick & Nelson Department Store. Off to the right of that entrance was Gene's Red Carpet Restaurant.

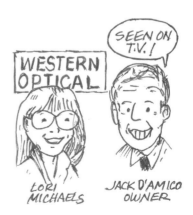

DOUG SHOWED ME THE
LEAD LINED ROOM.

The vacant office room in the new wing on the sixteenth floor had an eerie feeling. It was apparently used for x-rays in the early years. Doug collected some of the lead for melting into fishing sinkers. I still have a piece of lead.

Pipe breaks were common in the older side of the building. Water caused a lot of damage with bad smells from wet rugs, walls, plaster; and it took a while to clear up. We were required to carry extra insurance.

When the building had its own plumbers and electricians, John Green was one of them and attributed his longevity to electric shocks. He would touch two wires to see if there was a current. I learned from him not to be afraid of a few shocks when working around electricity.

In the 1960s we had a psychic cleaning lady with puffy lips named Rose. I was often working late so she would tell me things. She told me that a relative was about to die. It was always bad news. She knew when her ex-husband was passing.

Darlene worked years for Dr. Cloud. She was a nice looking girl and very proper. One day, I saw her in the hall. I'd just gotten off the elevator. She was doing a sort of dance. I had to ask what she was doing. She said, "I was just adjusting my panty hose!" Something I didn't know much about.

Karyn Markia graduated from Jenning's Dental School and has been in the building since 1967. She started at age eighteen. She worked a lot of those years for Dr. Amphlette, Helmer and McAuley.

Jackie Johnson was a striking redhead and a bookkeeper in our building's administrative office. One day in the eighties, she was on a break walking on the sidewalk when a car veered into her, and nearly killed her. It was touch and go! We all contributed to a fund to help out. She made it back to work until her retirement in the nineties.

As the building has aged, it has withstood earthquakes, fires, floods and changes in building codes. Late one night there was a fire in the Harrison Dental Lab on the second floor. Signs at the elevator said to use the stairs in case of fires. I tried the stairs, but they were full of smoke. Harrison Dental Lab was started by Clay Harrison. He was so pleasant and helpful. In the fifties before they moved out, they had as many as seventy technicians working in the lab.

Since then, the fire department had all the vents closed, including the rest room vents (can tell by the smell). They made us take off door props and further reduced ventilation that the original builders so valued. It caused the place to be cold and unfriendly. It's amazing how much we were able to see into an office as we walked by with the doors propped open. Even the mail slots eventually had to go. Progress has its trade offs. I wonder?

A guy with an accent started talking to me as we rode up in the elevator saying, "I'm starting a gold and jewelry business. I should do okay competing against these lazy Americans." Guess he thought I wasn't an American, but I also didn't appreciate what he was saying. Most of us with a small business were putting in long hours, six or seven days a week. He later moved out to the Bon Marche.

In May of 1992, Frederick & Nelson closed for good. They were a victim of a hostile take over. They were drained of their reserves and left to die. Later the Mayor helped Nordstrom buy the building. They remodeled it and brought it up to earthquake standards for about one hundred million dollars.

Moon's Café operated on the left side of the lobby for a few years in the 1990s. I liked her. She had this special persona that made the food taste better. She knew how to make customers feel good. She sold her place for a ridiculous price to open a bigger restaurant across the Sound. The second couple ran the place until the rent went up. That was a time of a lot of transitions. They moved to a spot near the Cinerama Theater.

A Korean couple ran the café on the second floor for a while until the building sold in 2005. I never understood why the man operated the cash register because women are usually better at greeting customers.

Lynn Pierce has been in the building since 1978. She is a Seattle Community College graduate and has worked for various dentists including Dr. Sondheim and Dr. Branch. She is currently working for Dr. Marvin who is married to Dr. Pat Fleege.

Kathleen Berry worked as an accountant for Speyer for years and has been a patient of Dr. Branch. She stopped by recently, and I learned she has worked for North Pacific Sea Foods the past eleven years. It turns out her current co-worker is Sam Nishikawa, who we've known for years along with his wife Hiroe. We've been recipients of special fish delicacies. Seattle is a small town and the connections are amazing.

There was a dental hygienist in the building with the French name Birdass (pronounced "birdouse"). Seems like she might have at least changed the spelling. I wonder if she married.

Aggie Smyth was outgoing and well known in the building when I came. She worked for Dr. Cox at the same time as Tom Enbody (he did a nice wax sculpture of her). She was proud of her 'perfect' nose and told everyone about her nose job. She met and married a wealthy man from Spokane. When the dental convention was in Spokane she had an elaborate party and invited all her dental friends.

In the 1970s, we had building plumbers. A colorful one was Marty. We kidded him about his big family and when his twelfth child was born, I remember how calm he was.

Pat McGowan runs an automatic concession machine business from Lacy to Bothell. He used to run the M-D Bldg Garage (1976-1991). It was a full service garage with fifty parking stalls. He still has the original garage safe. It took four men on the front of the truck to counterbalance it, while loading it. Parking was sixty-five dollars a month in 1991.

The Speyer boys sold their gold refining company and retired. It enabled D. J. Remlinger, who had worked for them, to open his own gold business, DJ also stands for dental and jewelry. Dennis came to the building shortly after me. He's led an interesting life, rafted the Grand Canyon, had a short marriage, and knows everyone. His family runs Remlinger Farms near Carnation.

The entrance to Frederick's was handy for all of us, especially during bad weather. Below was a stairwell that led to the basement and parking garage. The maintenance crew had a shop there for plumbers, electricians, and carpenters. There was even emergency water in big containers. Merlin Staatz was one of the quality crew.

In 2005, most of the second and third floors became a Health Club. The fourth and fifth floors are a soft-ware company, and the air conditioners were moved to the sixth floor.

Today, after the 2005 remodeling, the spacious lobby is about four times the original. The rest rooms are all wheelchair accessible, and they added to the halls. There are a lot of expensive extra spaces. These spaces are considered common areas. That means the occupants all pay because the percentage is figured according to the size of our offices.

The rest rooms, on each end of every floor, are bigger with a new latch that lights up red when occupied and green when vacant. We used to have personal keys but now they are open to the public (it may not last). The doctor across the hall became concerned when the rest room was occupied for hours. They found a bum asleep inside.

Current 2010 Businesses

My rent in 2010 is $663 for a small, one bay office facing the inside court. I see the back of Nordstrom, the top of the new cafeteria, and all the air conditioners. Actually, I get more done with the less interesting view.

The climbing wall is three stories high, taking up the empty space between Nordstrom and the M-D Bldg where the air-conditioner were moved up to create this new gathering place.

Dr. Bob Johnson Jr. and Dr. Irving Cohen enjoying lunch.

Bartell Drugs expanded to the corner, taking over Cold Stone Ice Cream store in 2010.

All Star Fitness, Downtown Executive Group X program has its entry on the ground floor and occupies most of the second and third floors.

After Western Optical and Kelley Ross moved out, Trudy's Flowers moved in. Since she signed a lease before the building was sold, they gave her a beautiful shop in the new lobby. It adds and gives color to the building. One Tuesday, I watched as Trudy watered flowers in a dental office. It's part of a service she gives when tenants buy her flowers to keep them looking good.

Since I am now
totally on cellular, it
has been convenient
to have this service
in the building on the
corner of Olive Way
and 6th Avenue.

TBC moved up from
Second Avenue and is
now a part of 'sway &
cake' which specializes in
women's fashion.

S.L.U.T. for South Lake Union Trolley is not the official
title, but probably the one that will stick. It was activated in
December 2007. The hope was to revive the downtown area
from Lake Union to the Westlake Station next to our M-D Bldg.
Seattle Electric Railway & Power Company originally laid the
tracks in 1890, and this project is a revival of those originally
laid along Westlake Avenue. I've used the streetcar one time
when Branch had an office party at a place on Lake Union.

MARIA DAILEY
PROPERTY
MANAGER

SARAH HUI
SR PROPERTY
MANAGER

PAIGE NORRIS
ASSISTANT
MANAGER

CURT HAMBLET
CHIEF ENGINEER

Now on the fourth floor, where I used to be, is ONVIA, an information company.
Its national headquarters is here on the fourth and fifth floors.

they have over 150 employees. I like the way they dressed up the elevator wall. It's insprirational, colorfu,l and bright. Wish we had more of that in the building.

Mildred Andrew, a Seattle writer, did a history of the M-D Bldg. that enabled the building to qualify for the National Registry of Historic Places and a Washington/city landmark. She gave me some of her notes. They've been very helpful. Other historic buildings are the Schaefer (1923), Dexter Horton (1922), Fourth & Pike (1925), Exchange (1929).

Amazing how much I depend on good mail, delivery and cleaning services every day just for my one-man, small office.

Pat the mailman is a history buff. His ancestors came over to the New World in 1520 with Cortez.

M-D Bldg Parking Garage in the basement is staffed by Diamond Parking. Anytime I'm walking past the entrance on 6th Avenue the loud speaker is always blasting.

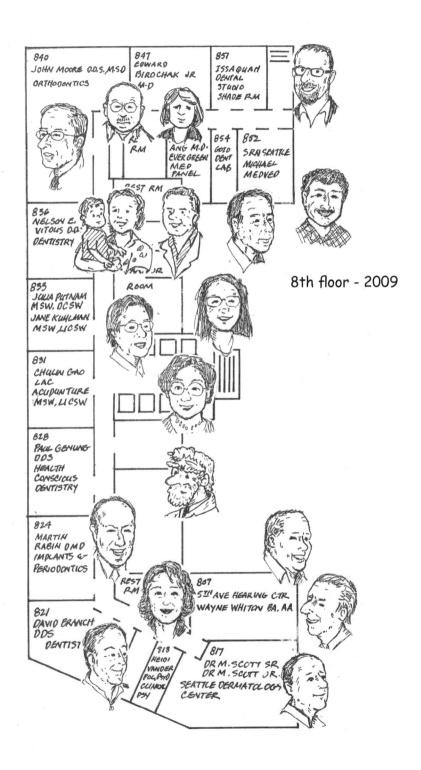

840
JOHN MOORE O.D.S. M.SD
ORTHODONTICS

847
EDWARD
BIROCHAK JR
M-D

851
ISSAQUAH
DENTAL
STUDIO
SHADE R.M

R.M

ANG M.D.
EVERGREEN
MED
PANEL

854
GOTO
DENT
LAB

852
SRN SEATTLE
MICHAEL
MEDVED

REST RM

836
NELSON E.
VITOUS D.D.
DENTISTRY

ROOM

833
JULIA PUTNAM
MSW. OCSW
JANE KUHLMAN
MSW, LICSW

8th floor - 2009

831
CHULIN GAO
LAC
ACUPUNTURE
MSW, LICSW

828
PAUL GENUNG
DDS
HEALTH
CONSCIOUS
DENTISTRY

824
MARTIN
RABIN DMD
IMPLANTS &
PERIODONTICS

821
DAVID BRANCH
DDS
DENTIST

REST
R.M

807
5TH AVE HEARING CTR
WAYNE WHITON BA, AA

818
HE101
VANDER
FOLPSYD
CLINICL
PSY

817
DR M.SCOTT SR
DR M.SCOTT JR.
SEATTLE DERMATOLOGY
CENTER

13
Conclusion

Here I am in my den working on my book in our daylight basement which also serves as a guest room with a wall bed that converts to a table so I can spread out. the "Kelly" cats visit often.

From the ceiling, in front of the Marv Herard nude, is my army dogtag: US56-253-310. To the right, hanging from the ceiling, is an onion weeder we used on the farm in the 1940s and 1950s. Under the "stamp" art by Al Capp and Chester Gould is a piranha fish from our Iquitos, Peru, trip, a gooey duck, an empty Kentucky Fried Chicken tub, and stuff for this book. Above the radio is a Napoleon Hill quote, then the "Desert Rat" I drew in the army. Some GIs had it tattooed. Plenty of inconsequential treasures!

The number "13" has played an interesting role in my life. I was delivered by a midwife at 1303 Washington Street in Seattle, at 3 a.m., on Friday the 13th on 1/13/33. The last four digits of my army serial no. 3310, with three and one, was used as a laundry ID. Therefore, 13 chapters in this project.

In 1976, after eighteen years of bowling on Thursday nights, I quit. My goal was to hit a 300 game and a 700 series; I never made it. No matter, if I was doing good or bad, I ended up hitting my average. I've learned my subconscious mind kept me there. I wanted more in life.

An army buddy had gotten me interested in Real Estate, so in 1976 I took a George Hawkins Real Estate Seminar and learned that inflation would help make payments easier and rent could keep up. I ended up buying two fixer uppers for about twenty thousand dollars each. I enjoyed remodeling and fixing. Since I owned my own business, I also needed something for retirement.

The Hawkins Seminar got me going with personal growth and self-improvement. A group of ten, including George Hawkins, researched the best ways to earn extra money for investing in Real Estate and came up with Shaklee Company. It was a company with a sales plan that paid the most returns, with well-researched products as the best. It had a philosophy (the very early beginning of "green" and "wellness" movements), and I had also heard about Shaklee on radio.

It turned out the CEO of Shaklee, Gary Shansby, was a fishing buddy of my doctor in our building, Dr. N. Arcese, who said to me, "Don't get everyone healthy till I retire." It was Dr. Arcese's advice that I was close to being diagnosed with diabetes that got me researching natural ways of managing my condition with Shaklee Nutrition. When I was visiting the dentist, Dr. Loomis, around that time, I noticed on his shelf boxes of before and after models

of George Hawkin's full mouth restoration case. Dr. Gallaher also knew Gary Shansby and Arcese from Queen Anne High School. Strange, the connections in life.

As a result of this new direction in my life, I studied Napoleon Hill's book Think and Grow Rich which was recommended by most of the gurus in personal enrichment. The secret in the book is to concentrate one's thoughts on developing self-confidence, determine one's chief aim in life, and become a self reliant and successful person. One must truly believe he or she can.

I've come to realize we are born with certain talents. We are born with characteristics like the color of one's skin, hair and eyes. We can improve but can't go much beyond a set point. There is a lot of room for improvement to get to the set point, but there are a few things that have to wait for another lifetime. Right? We are born with certain talents that make us strong and weaknesses that keep us humble.

Under the cover of my casting machine are written some affirmations like "A negative attitude toward others will never bring me success!" They remind me, as I melt gold, of things that I've learned so far in my journey through life and how much more there is.

There was an incident when Dr. Sproule sent Norman Davis down to see me. He was a coin expert and had a rare Greek collection at the Seattle Art Museum. He noticed a jigsaw puzzle I had pasted on to a cupboard door, and I usually opened the door to hide the Playboy centerfold when people came in. He reprimanded me! He was very proper.

There is so much to learn. I've read some good books that make me think. I agree with most of Ayn Rand's philosophy. Our daughter, Kelly, worked with Lou Tice, and his tapes were very good. It's been fun. I trust that some of it will stay in my subconscious and continue to help me grow.

Of interest is the Cascadia earth subduction of January 1700, causing a massive tsunami that affected our area. Here on Mercer Island ancient cedar trees lie deeply off shore in Lake Washington, thought to be part of that event.

I used to see a lot of starlings on the way to my parking lot during warm summer months. A cloud of black would descend on certain trees. As I watched, amid a canopy of chirps and confusion, they seemed to be vying for king of the tree. Then they would settle down for the night, leaving poop all around. Don't see them much any more. Wonder why.

Stuff that baffles me are things like mathematics. I don't understand how, with equations, some are able to prove their theories. And then, there is music. How do musicians know what key or note to hit before they hear it? How are athletes able to calculate the speed of the ball and know how fast to run? Life is full of mysteries.

I've always had interest in economics, but in college, I almost flunked economics because of a misunderstanding. The professor was from Austria and had a strong accent, so I had a hard time understanding what he wanted. He also accused me of copying. I met him on campus one day and talked it out. Instead of getting a red card for doing bad or a green card for doing good, I got no card.

In Atlas Shrugged, Ayn Rand shows how the value producers hold up the economy as well as the government. Honesty is important. I don't care for her anti religion thoughts, but no one person is right on everything. It gives me food for thought.

When the girls were in college, Dee went back to get her Master's Degree in Psychosocial Nursing and Stress Management. She wrote her thesis on The Difference Between Men & Women and How They Use Social Support. One of the conclusions is that both men and woman prefer women to talk out their problems with. Then there is the "Savior Syndrome" where people that are helped often grow to resent their saviors. Interesting!

We've all heard it said, "Man was made with free will." But to have free will, we need freedom of choice. To have freedom of choice, we need democracy. Thomas Sowell teaches this principle he learned from his own instructors. This helps me value the big picture and not just the perfect tooth contact on a bridge.

HSP, highly sensitive people, coined and described by Dr. Elaine N. Aron in 1996, is thought to affect a fifth of our population. Shyness, inhibition and fearfulness have been considered a deficiency, but Aron suggest these people process sensory information more deeply and thoroughly. HSP's brains are wired differently.

I consider myself an HSP, and maybe it helps me be more artistic. I wish I wasn't so sensitive at times when I have too many bridges with deadlines that make me feel overwhelmed; or when I have to psych myself up to give a talk. I learned the fundamentals of giving an interesting talk, but I think I'll stick to drawing and making teeth.

I'm in good company. I consider brilliant people like Dr. Jeffrey Bland from our Nutrition Study Club an HSP. An example of a well known HSP is Charles Darwin; he was a genius. It is good to understand some of these things about myself and helps me understand others. It also helps me be a more understanding parent and grandparent. So HSPs watch your p's and q's and let your creativity flow.

I learned it's best to talk directly to the doctor. The more people it goes through the worse it sounds.

In the 1980s, we had Sheryn Hara teach us a course on P.E.T. (Parent Effectiveness Training). We learned how best to use "I" language. It was one of the first classes I'd taken, and it has turned out to be one of the most useful courses I ever took.

"You" is a put-down, especially during problem times.

"I" takes responsibility (when used correctly).

Bad "you" language is particularly a problem. She was attractive, but her use of "you" seemed bossy and bitchy. She was always right. No wonder she was let go.

Some of the funnest times were the toughest times. The 1970s and the 1980s were busy; the kids needing more money for college and cars made it tough. We made our mortgages, but had to borrow some for college. Looking back, it was fun and Dee managed to stay at home for most of the time.

Part of what got me through the tough times was learning about nutrition. I remember feeling so bad one day, I felt like jumping out my fourth floor window when I was installing the air- conditioner. After a Glucose Tolerance Test, Dr. Arcese informed me that I was heading toward diabetes. My dad had diabetes.

That's when I joined the Nutrition Study Club started by Dr. Sondheim in the seventeenth floor conference room once a month. I talked Dee into starting a home-based counseling and Shaklee business with her degrees in psychosocial nursing and nutrition. As a result, I've avoided a Diabetes diagnosis for thirty-plus years.

In the early eighties at a nutrition seminar, Dee showed me her notes and the "Story of the Healthy Cell" was born. We've learned a lot but it's still a minute part of natural ways of healing ourselves.

Solid science as well as experience is proving there is a difference between natural and synthetic.

It may not be fasionable
but it seems;
that we should live within our means.

I've lived with no electricity, no plumbing, no money but its been fun. If we have as many changes in the next seventy-seven years, as I've seen in the last seventy-seven, it should be exciting and worth tough times.

Cause and effect, reincarnation and karma make sense to me. Could be that we are responsible for being here at this time. Maybe we choose to be born into these circumstances. It is also becoming more clear that being born into wealth also has its own challenges.

If we chose to be born into this time slot, there must be a reason. Our souls are hopefully learning lessons from this incarnation. Maybe it's as simple as that!

As we age I like to think:
Growing old is not a sin;
Life's boat we're all in.

I worked a lot of late nights during the early years. Now, if I'm down town late, when it's quiet and the air is cool, I get a nostalgic feeling. We technicians all worked late. I remember Bill Malone, of Moss Malone Dental lab, was killed when he drove into a road barrier. It was usually open but had been closed because it was so late.

I recall working all night on a bridge due at 8:00 A.M. and just finishing it before the dentist arrived. It was normal to get a midnight call from a fellow tech. In the seventies there was talk of unionizing so we could have better hours but nothing came of it. It would have increased the cost of dentistry.

As I conclude this book, I realize:

Tomorrow becomes today
Today becomes yesterday and
Yesterday becomes history.
There is no end to history.

A final thought:
To do what's right
is hard to do,
When no one knows
but God and you.

THANKS & GOOD LUCK!
—GG